ROYAL COURT

Royal Court Theatre presents

NIGHTSONGS

by **Jon Fosse**
translated by Gregory Motton

First performance at the Royal Court Jerwood Theatre Downstairs
Sloane Square, London on 21 February 2002.

Nightsongs is supported by the Quercus Trust

NIGHTSONGS

by **Jon Fosse**
translated by Gregory Motton

Cast
Jonathan Cullen
Gillian Hanna
Paul Higgins
Sophie Okonedo
Christopher Saul

Director **Katie Mitchell**
Lighting Designer **Paule Constable**
Sound Designer **Gareth Fry**
Artistic Consultant **Antoni Malinowski**
Casting Director **Lisa Makin**
Production Manager **Paul Handley**
Company Stage Manager **Cath Binks**
Stage Manager **Pea Horsley**
Stage Management Work Placement **Laura Farrell**
Costume Supervisor **Iona Kenrick**
Company Voice Work **Patsy Rodenburg**

Royal Court Theatre would like to thank the following for their help with this production:
Steve Tompkins, Andy Hales, Iona Kenrick, John Cullen, The Cloth House, www.natrahealth.com, Mattel Inc (www.mattel.com), Baby List Co. (www.babylist.co.uk), Rosebys (www.rosebys.com),
Wardrobe care by Persil and Comfort courtesy of Lever Fabergé.

THE COMPANY

Jon Fosse (writer)
Theatre includes (productions in 2001 and 2002): The Child (Thalia, Hamburg/Neues Theatre, Schauspielhalle); Visits (Théâtre d'Avignon/ Helsingborgs Stadsteater); Dream of Autumn (Burgtheater, Akademietheater, Wien/Odense Teater/Schaübuhne, Berlin/Kammerspiele, Munich/ Staatstheater Darmstadt/Bühnen der Stadt Köln/ Katona Josef Teater, Budapest/ Dramaten, Stockholm/Tröndelag Teater/Artistas Unidos, Lisbon/St. Petersburg/Israel/Slovakia); Afternoon (Teaterhøgskolen i Oslo/Stockholms Teater högskola/ Riksteatret, Oslo); Closed Guitar (Den Nationale Scene, Bergen); And Never We'll Be Parted (Teatre Malic, Barcelona); A Summer's Day (Festival Lire en Fête, Paris/Festival Off d'Avignon Palace Theatre/Svenska Teatern, Helsingfors/ Compagnie pour memoire, Paris/Bastille, Paris/ Théâtre Vidy, Lausanne/Palace Theatre, Essex/ Island); The Guitar Man (Schauspielhaus, Zurich/ Essen/Galeasen, Stockholm); Melancholia (Ateliers Contemporaines/Théâtre de la Colline, Paris/ Haugesund Teater); Mother and Child (Teater Giljotin, Stockholm/Folketearet, Copenhagen/ Serbia); The Name (Théâtre Vidy, Lausanne/ Théâtre National de Strasbourg/Théâtre de la Tempête, Paris/The Salzburg Festival/The National Theatre, Riga/Kajna Theatre/Théâtre de la Colline/ Düsseldorf Schauspielhaus/Landestheater, Linz/ Schaübuhne, Berlin/ Schaübuhne at the Festival in Ponti/Theater Freiburg/Wesfälische Kammerspiele, Paderborn/Theater Munster/Theater Graz/Theater Heidelberg/Schauspielhaus, Bonn/Pfalztheater Kaiserslautern/Neue Bühne Senftenberg/ Studiobühne Bayreuth/Theater Regnsberg/Teater Zep, Amsterdam/Polski Theatre, Worchlav); Nightsongs (Théâtre du Grand Midi, Bruxelles/Les Perles de Verre, Montpellier/Kammerspiele Magdeburg/Saaländisches Staatstheater, Saabrüchen /Staatstheater Mainz/Landestheater Detmold/ Theater Nürnberg/Teater Aachen/Bühnen der Landeshauptstadt, Kiel/Schauspiel Leipzig/Theater Zep, Amsterdam/Schauspielhaus, Zürich/ Staatsschauspiel, Dresden); Someone Is Going to Come (Volkstheater, Vienna/Theatre Rideau du Bruxelles/Publiekstheater, Gent/RHO Fabrica de Sueños, Santiago/The National Theatre, Brno/ Ateliers Contemporaines, Paris/ Statstheater, Darmstadt/Düsseldorfer Schauspielhaus/Städtishe Buhnen Frankfurt, Statstheater, Hannover/Aeoria, Athens/Theatre festival in Rome/Nationaltheatret, Oslo/A Capital, Lisbon/Sala Beckett, Barcelona); Sleep You Little Child of Mine (Theatre Gerard Philippe, Paris/Det Norske Teatret, Oslo); The Son (Théatre de Léscouade/ Prétexte, Region de Troyes/Théatre de Volcan, Le Havre); Winter (Rialto, Copenhagen/Ålborg Teater/Schauspielhaus Zürich); Death Variations (Nationaltheatret, Oslo).
Awards include: The Ibsen Prize for The Name.
Jon has also written numerous novels, children's books, volumes of poetry and essays.

Paule Constable (lighting designer)
For the Royal Court: Boy Gets Girl, Mountain Language/Ashes To Ashes, Presence, Credible Witness, The Country, Dublin Carol, The Weir, The Glory of Living.
Other theatre includes: The Seagull, Tales from Ovid, The Dispute, Uncle Vanya, Beckett Shorts, The Mysteries (RSC); The Villains' Opera, Darker Face of the Earth, Haroun and the Sea of Stories, Caucasian Chalk Circle (RNT); Amadeus (West End, Broadway, Olivier nomination); Vagina Monologues (West End); The Servant (Lyric); More Grimms' Tales (Young Vic and New York); four productions for Theatre de Complicite including the Olivier-nominated Street of Crocodiles.
Opera includes: productions for the Royal Opera House, English National Opera, Welsh National Opera, Scottish Opera, Opera North, Glyndebourne, La Monnaie.

Jonathan Cullen
For the Royal Court: Under the Blue Sky, Our Late Night, Rafts and Dreams, Gibraltar Straight, Falkland Sound, The Wall Dog.
Other theatre includes: Albert Speer, Ghetto, Fuente Ovejuna, Bartholomew Fair, Strangeness of Others (RNT); Our Country's Good (Young Vic/Out of Joint); Grace Note (Old Vic); The Merchant of Venice (Sheffield Crucible); Desire Under the Elms (Shared Experience); Vieux Carré (Nottingham Playhouse); Morning & Evening (Hampstead); Feelgood (Hampstead/West End); The Clandestine Marriage (Queens); Miss Julie (Salisbury Playhouse); Venice Preserv'd (Royal Exchange, Manchester); Dr Faustus (Greenwich); Chatsky (Almeida); 'Tis Pity She's a Whore, A Woman Kill'd With Kindness (RSC); Widowers' Houses (Palace, Watford).
Television and film includes: The Innocents, The Echo, The Unknown Soldier, Crossing the Floor, Dalziel & Pascoe, Henry IV, Between the Lines, Calling the Shots, Headhunters, Inspector Alleyn, A Woman at War, 1914 All Out, Robin Hood.

Gareth Fry (sound designer)
For the Royal Court: Redundant, Mountain Language/Ashes To Ashes, The Country.
Other theatre includes: Accrington Pals (Chichester); The Oresteia (RNT); Noise of Time, Mnemonic, The Street of Crocodiles (Theatre de Complicite); Wexford Trilogy (Oxford Stage Company).

Gillian Hanna
For the Royal Court: Fireface, Hot Fudge and Ice Cream, Stranger's House; Road (1994) and The Queen and I (with Out of Joint); East is East (with Tamasha/Theatre Royal Stratford East).
Other theatre includes: The Caucasian Chalk Circle, Braddocks Time (Everyman, Liverpool); Teen Dreams, Calamity Jane, Gentlemen Prefer Blonds, Kiss and Kill, Vinegar Tom, Scum: Death, Destruction and Dirty Washing, Origin of the Species (Monstrous Regiment); City Echoes, Sweeny Todd, Tale of Two Cities (Liverpool Playhouse); Sweeny Todd, Destiny, Spend Spend Spend, Elizabeth, Almost by Chance a Woman (Half Moon); Duet for One (Crucible); The House of Bernada Alba (Lyric Hammersmith); Curtains (Hampstead Theatre); Wuthering Heights, Who's Afraid of Virginia Woolf, A Common Woman, Leonce and Lena (Crucible, Sheffield); Juno and the Paycock (Contact, Manchester); Wallflowering (West Yorkshire Playhouse); Romeo and Juliet, A View From the Bridge (Royal Exchange); Big Maggie (Birmingham Rep); A Passionate Woman (Leicester Haymarket); Emma (Edinburgh Festival and Tricycle); Ariadne Auf Naxos (Edinburgh Festival Theatre); Medea (Queens).
Television includes: Brookside, Horizon, All Creatures Great and Small, Making News, Sweet Sixteen, The Roughest Way, House of Bernada Alba, Poirot, The Marshall, The Story of Phillip Knight, Desmonds, Brookside, Drop the Dead Donkey, The Heart Surgeon, Dangerfield, All the Queen's Men, Where the Heart Is.
Film includes: Wolves of Willoughby Chase, The Woman and the Wolf, Les Miserables, Best.

Paul Higgins
For the Royal Court: Conquest of the South Pole, American Bagpipes, A Wholly Healthy Glasgow (also Royal Exchange, Manchester).
Other theatre includes: The Birthday Party (Shared Experience); A View From the Bridge, Romeo and Juliet, The Odd Women, The Way of the World (Royal Exchange, Manchester); The Hare Trilogy, An Enemy of the People (RNT); The Lady From the Sea (Lyric Hammersmith and West Yorkshire Playhouse); Slab Boys Trilogy (Young Vic); The Maidenstone, Buried Alive (Hampstead); Macbeth (English Touring Co. and Lyric Hammersmith); Conversations After a Burial (Almeida).
Television includes: The Negotiator, A Wholly Healthy Glasgow, A Very Peculiar Practice, Tumbledown, Dr Finlay, Staying Alive, Beating Jesus, Murder.
Film includes: Bedrooms and Hallways, Complicity.
Writing for television: Opera Lovers and Peripheral Vision for the Series Table 12.

Katie Mitchell (director)
For the Royal Court: Mountain Language/Ashes To Ashes, The Country.
Other theatre includes: A Woman Killed With Kindness, The Dybbuk, Ghosts, Henry VI, Easter, Phoenician Woman, The Mysteries, Beckett Shorts, Uncle Vanya (with The Young Vic) (RSC); Rutherford and Son, The Machine Wreckers, The Oresteia (RNT); Iphigenia at Aulis, The Last Ones (Abbey Dublin); Endgame (Donmar Warehouse); Attempts On Her Life (Piccolo Teatro di Milano); The Maids (Young Vic).
Opera includes: Don Giovanni, Jenufa and Katya Kabanova (Welsh National Opera).
Awards include: 1996 Evening Standard Award for Best Director for The Phoenician Woman (RSC).

Gregory Motton (translator)
Translations of other Jon Fosse plays includes: The Name, Someone is Going to Come.
Other translations include: Creditors, The Friends, Miss Julie, The Father, Ghost Sonata, Swanwhite, The Pelican, The Dance of Death, The Storm, The Burned Site.
Gregory is currently working on a four volume collection of 24 of Strindberg's plays for Oberon Books.
As a playwright, theatre includes: Ambulance, Downfall, The Terrible Voice of Satan (Royal Court); Looking at You (revived) Again (Leicester Haymarket); A Message for the Broken Hearted (Liverpool Playhouse); Cat and Mouse (Sheep), In Praise of Progress (Theatre de L'Odeon, Paris); A Little Satire (Gate); God's Island (Paris Villette).

Sophie Okonedo
For the Royal Court: I Just Stopped By To See The Man, Been So Long.
Other theatre includes: Troilus and Cressida, Money (RNT); Arabian Nights (Young Vic); His Lordship's Fancy (Gate); A Jovial Crew, The Odyssey, Tamburlaine the Great, The Changeling (RSC); 900 Oneonta (Old Vic).
Television includes: Never Never, Clocking Off, Sweet Revenge, Staying Alive, Deep Secrets, Maria's Child.
Film includes: This Year's Love, The Jackal, Go Now, Ace Ventura II, Miss Queencake, Dirty, Pretty Things.
Radio includes: Pocahontas, Richard III, Timbuktu.

Christopher Saul
Theatre includes: Servant to Two Masters (RSC and West End); Richard II, Henry IV, Part I & II, Comedy of Errors, Columbus, Theban Plays, Breaking the Silence, Merry Wives, Richard III, Hamlet (RSC); Twelfth Night (Acter); More Grimm Tales (Young Vic and New York); As I Lay Dying, Twelfth Night, The Ancient Mariner, Start Right (Young Vic); Romeo and Juliet, Comedy of Errors (English Shakespeare Company); A Variety of Death Defying Acts (Orange Tree).
Television includes: Coronation Street, Sharman, London's Burning, Grange Hill, Castles, 99-1, Between the Lines, Rides, The Chief, Waterfront Beat, Never Come Back, Chain, One Foot in the Grave, Small Zones, Poirot, Casualty, Watching, Brookside, Triangle, Game Set & Match, The Bill, Simon and the Witch.
Film includes: Wilt, Mountbatten: The Last Viceroy.

THE ENGLISH STAGE COMPANY AT THE ROYAL COURT

The English Stage Company at the Royal Court opened in 1956 as a subsidised theatre producing new British plays, international plays and some classical revivals.

The first artistic director George Devine aimed to create a writers' theatre, 'a place where the dramatist is acknowledged as the fundamental creative force in the theatre and where the play is more important than the actors, the director, the designer'. The urgent need was to find a contemporary style in which the play, the acting, direction and design are all combined. He believed that 'the battle will be a long one to continue to create the right conditions for writers to work in'.

Devine aimed to discover 'hard-hitting, uncompromising writers whose plays are stimulating, provocative and exciting'. The Royal Court production of John Osborne's Look Back in Anger in May 1956 is now seen as the decisive starting point of modern British drama and the policy created a new generation of British playwrights. The first wave included John Osborne, Arnold Wesker, John Arden, Ann Jellicoe, N F Simpson and Edward Bond. Early seasons included new international plays by Bertolt Brecht, Eugène Ionesco, Samuel Beckett, Jean-Paul Sartre and Marguerite Duras.

The theatre started with the 400-seat proscenium arch Theatre Downstairs, and then in 1969 opened a second theatre, the 60-seat studio Theatre Upstairs. Some productions transfer to the West End, such as Caryl Churchill's Far Away, Conor McPherson's The Weir, Kevin Elyot's Mouth to Mouth and My Night With Reg. The Royal Court also co-produces plays which have transferred to the West End or toured internationally, such as Sebastian Barry's The Steward of Christendom and Mark Ravenhill's Shopping and Fucking (with Out of Joint), Martin McDonagh's The Beauty Queen Of Leenane (with Druid Theatre Company), Ayub Khan-Din's East is East (with Tamasha Theatre Company, and now a feature film).

Since 1994 the Royal Court's artistic policy has again been vigorously directed to finding and producing a new generation of playwrights. The writers include Joe Penhall, Rebecca Prichard, Michael Wynne, Nick Grosso, Judy Upton, Meredith Oakes, Sarah Kane, Anthony Neilson, Judith Johnson, James Stock, Jez Butterworth, Marina Carr, Simon Block, Martin McDonagh, Mark Ravenhill, Ayub Khan-Din, Tamantha Hammerschlag, Jess Walters, Che Walker, Conor McPherson, Simon Stephens, Richard Bean, Roy

photo: Andy Chopping

Williams, Gary Mitchell, Mick Mahoney, Rebecca Gilman, Christopher Shinn, Kia Corthron, David Gieselmann, Marius von Mayenburg, David Eldridge, Leo Butler, Zinnie Harris, Grae Cleugh, Roland Schimmelpfennig and Vassily Sigarev. This expanded programme of new plays has been made possible through the support of A.S.K Theater Projects, the Jerwood Charitable Foundation, the American Friends of the Royal Court Theatre and many in association with the Royal National Theatre Studio.

In recent years there have been record-breaking productions at the box office, with capacity houses for Jez Butterworth's Mojo, Sebastian Barry's The Steward of Christendom, Martin McDonagh's The Beauty Queen of Leenane, Ayub Khan-Din's East is East, Eugène Ionesco's The Chairs, David Hare's My Zinc Bed and Conor McPherson's The Weir, which transferred to the West End in October 1998 and ran for nearly two years at the Duke of York's Theatre.

The newly refurbished theatre in Sloane Square opened in February 2000, with a policy still inspired by the first artistic director George Devine. The Royal Court is an international theatre for new plays and new playwrights, and the work shapes contemporary drama in Britain and overseas.

REBUILDING THE ROYAL COURT

In 1995, the Royal Court was awarded a National Lottery grant through the Arts Council of England, to pay for three quarters of a £26m project to completely rebuild its 100-year old home. The rules of the award required the Royal Court to raise £7.6m in partnership funding. The building has been completed thanks to the generous support of those listed below.

We are particularly grateful for the contributions of over 5,700 audience members.

English Stage Company Registered Charity number 231242.

ROYAL COURT DEVELOPMENT BOARD
Tamara Ingram (Chair)
Jonathan Cameron (Vice Chair)
Timothy Burrill
Anthony Burton
Jonathan Caplan QC
Deborah Davis
Cecily Engle
Kimberly Fortier
Julia Hobsbawm
Joyce Hytner
Mary Ellen Johnson
Dan Klein
Michael Potter
Mark Robinson
William Russell
Sue Stapely
James L Tanner

PRINCIPAL DONOR
Jerwood Foundation

WRITERS CIRCLE
The Cadogan Estate
Carillon/Schal
News International plc
Pathé
The Eva and Hans K Rausing Trust
The Rayne Foundation
Sky
Garfield Weston Foundation

DIRECTORS CIRCLE
The Esmée Fairbairn Foundation
The Granada Group plc

ACTORS CIRCLE
Edwin C Cohen & The Blessing Way Foundation
Sir Ronald Cohen & Sharon Harel-Cohen
Quercus Charitable Trust
The Basil Samuel Charitable Trust
The Trusthouse Charitable Foundation
The Woodward Charitable Trust

SPECIFIC DONATIONS
The Foundation for Sport and the Arts for Stage System
John Lewis Partnership plc for Balcony
City Parochial Foundation for Infra Red Induction Loops and Toilets for Disabled Patrons
RSA Art for Architecture Award Scheme for Antoni Malinowski Wall Painting

THE AMERICAN FRIENDS OF THE ROYAL COURT THEATRE

AFRCT support the mission of the Royal Court and are primarily focused on raising funds to enable the theatre to produce new work by emerging American writers. Since this not-for-profit organisation was founded in 1997, AFRCT has contributed to seven productions including Rebecca Gilman's Boy Gets Girl. They have also supported the participation of young artists in the Royal Court's acclaimed International Residency.

If you would like to support the ongoing work of the Royal Court, please contact the Development Department on 020 7565 5050.

AMERICAN FRIENDS

Founders
Harry Brown
Victoria Elenowitz
Francis Finlay
Monica Gerard-Sharp
The Howard Gilman Foundation
Jeananne Hauswald
Mary Ellen Johnson
Dany Khosrovani
Kay Koplovitz
The Laura Pels Foundation
The Magowan Family Foundation
Monica Menell-Kinberg Ph.D.
Benjamin Rauch
Rory Riggs
Robert Rosenkranz
Gerald Schoenfeld, The Shubert Organization

Patrons
Daniel Baudendistel
Arthur Bellinzoni
Miriam Bienstock
Robert L & Janice Billingsley
Catherine G Curran
Leni Darrow
Michael & Linda Donovan
Ursula & William Fairbairn
April Foley
Amanda Foreman
Mr & Mrs Richard Gelfond
Mr & Mrs Richard Grand
Mr & Mrs Paul Hallingby
Sharon King Hoge
The Carl C Icahn Family Foundation
Maurice & Jean R Jacobs
Mr & Mrs Ernest Kafka
Sahra T Lese
Susan & Martin Lipton
Eleanor Margolis
Hamish & Georgone Maxwell
Kathleen O'Grady
Howard & Barbara Sloan
Margaret Jackson Smith
Mika Sterling
Arielle Tepper
The Thorne Foundation

Benefactors
Mr & Mrs Tom Armstrong
Mr & Mrs Mark Arnold
Elaine Attias
Rachael Bail
Mr & Mrs Matthew Chapman
David Day
Richard & Rosalind Edelman
Abe & Florence Elenowitz
Hiram & Barbara Gordon
Mr & Mrs Brian Keelan
Jennifer C E Laing
Burt Lerner
Imelda Liddiard
Dr Anne Locksley
Mr & Mrs Rudolph Rauch
Lawrence & Helen Remmel
Mr & Mrs Robert Rosenberg
Mr & Mrs William Russell
Harold Sanditen
Mr & Mrs Robert Scully
Julie Talen
Mr & Mrs Charles Whitman

American Friends Development Director
Timothy Runion
Tel: (212) 408 0465

THE ARTS COUNCIL OF ENGLAND

PROGRAMME SUPPORTERS

The Royal Court (English Stage Company Ltd) receives its principal funding from London Arts. It is also supported financially by a wide range of private companies and public bodies and earns the remainder of its income from the box office and its own trading activities.
The Royal Borough of Kensington & Chelsea gives an annual grant to the Royal Court Young Writers' Programme and the London Boroughs Grants Committee provides project funding for a number of play development initiatives.

The Jerwood Charitable Foundation continues to support new plays by new playwrights through the Jerwood New Playwrights series. Since 1993 the A.S.K. Theater Projects of Los Angeles has funded a Playwrights' Programme at the theatre. Bloomberg Mondays, the Royal Court's reduced price ticket scheme, is supported by Bloomberg.

TRUSTS AND FOUNDATIONS
American Friends of the Royal Court Theatre
Anon
The Carnegie United Kingdom Trust
Carlton Television Trust
Gerald Chapman Fund
The Foundation for Sport and the Arts
Genesis Foundation
The Goldsmiths' Company
Jerwood Charitable Foundation
John Lyon's Charity
The Laura Pels Foundation
Quercus Charitable Trust
The Peggy Ramsay Foundation
The Peter Jay Sharp Foundation
The Royal Victoria Hall Foundation
The Sobell Foundation
The Trusthouse Charitable Foundation
Garfield Weston Foundation

MAJOR SPONSORS
Amerada Hess
A.S.K. Theater Projects
AT&T: *OnStage*
BBC
Bloomberg
Channel Four
Royal College of Psychiatrists

BUSINESS MEMBERS
BP
CGNU plc
J Walter Thompson
Lazard
Lever Fabergé
McCABES
Pemberton Greenish
Peter Jones
Redwood
SIEMENS
Simons Muirhead & Burton

INDIVIDUAL MEMBERS
Patrons
Anon
Advanpress
Katie Bradford
Mark Bentley
Mrs Alan Campbell-Johnson
David Coppard
Chris Corbin
David Day
Thomas Fenton
Ralph A Fields
John Flower
Edna & Peter Goldstein
Homevale Ltd
Tamara Ingram
Mr & Mrs Jack Keenan
Barbara Minto
New Penny Productions Ltd
Martin Newson
AT Poeton & Son Ltd.
André Ptaszynski, Really Useful Theatres
Caroline Quentin
William & Hilary Russell
Ian & Carol Sellars
Miriam Stoppard
Carl & Martha Tack
Jan & Michael Topham
Mr & Mrs Anthony Weldon
Richard Wilson OBE
Amanda Vail

Benefactors
Anon
Anastasia Alexander
Lesley E Alexander
Judith Asalache
Batia Asher
Mr & Mrs J Attard-Manché
Elaine Mitchell Attias
Matilde Attolico
Thomas Bendhem
Keith & Helen Bolderson
Jeremy Bond
Brian Boylan
Mr & Mrs F H Bradley III
Mrs Elly Brook JP
Julian Brookstone
Paul & Ossi Burger
Debbi & Richard Burston
Yuen-Wei Chew
Martin Cliff
Carole & Neville Conrad
Conway Van Gelder
Coppard & Co.
Barry Cox
Curtis Brown Ltd
Peter Czernin
Deborah Davis
Chris & Jane Deering
Zöe Dominic
Robyn Durie
Lorraine Esdaile
Winston & Jean Fletcher
Nick Fraser
Jacqueline & Jonathan Gestetner
Michael Goddard
Carolyn Goldbart
Judy & Frank Grace
Byron Grote
Sue & Don Guiney
Hamilton Asper Management
Woodley Hapgood
Jan Harris
Phil Hobbs
Amanda Howard Associates
Mrs Martha Hummer-Bradley
Lisa Irwin-Burgess
Mr & Mrs T Kassem
Paul Kaju & Jane Peterson
Peter & Maria Kellner
Diana King
Clico Kingsbury
Lee & Thompson
Caroline & Robert Lee
Carole A Leng
Lady Lever
Colette & Peter Levy
Ann Lewis
Ian Mankin
Christopher Marcus
David Marks
Alan & Tricia Marshall
Nicola McFarland
Mr & Mrs Roderick R McManigal
Mae Modiano
Eva Monley
Pat Morton
Georgia Oetker
Paul Oppenheimer
Janet & Michael Orr
Diana Parker
Maria Peacock
Pauline Pinder
Jeremy Priestley
John & Rosemarie Reynolds
Samuel French Ltd
Bernice & Victor Sandelson
John Sandoe (Books) Ltd
Nicholas Selmes
Bernard Shapero
Jenny Sheridan
Lois Sieff OBE
Peregrine Simon
Brian D Smith
John Soderquist
The Spotlight
Max Stafford-Clark
Sue Stapely
June Summerill
Anthony Wigram
George & Moira Yip
Georgia Zaris

STAGE HANDS CIRCLE
Graham Billing
Andrew Cryer
Lindy Fletcher
Susan Hayden
Mr R Hopkins
Philip Hughes Trust
Dr A V Jones
Roger Jospe
Miss A Lind-Smith
Mr J Mills
Nevin Charitable Trust
Janet & Michael Orr
Jeremy Priestley
Ann Scurfield
Brian Smith
Harry Streets
Thai Ping Wong
Richard Wilson OBE
C C Wright

LBG LONDON ARTS

AWARDS FOR THE ROYAL COURT

Terry Johnson's Hysteria won the 1994 Olivier Award for Best Comedy, and also the Writers' Guild Award for Best West End Play. Kevin Elyot's My Night with Reg won the 1994 Writers' Guild Award for Best Fringe Play, the Evening Standard Award for Best Comedy, and the 1994 Olivier Award for Best Comedy. Joe Penhall was joint winner of the 1994 John Whiting Award for Some Voices. Sebastian Barry won the 1995 Writers' Guild Award for Best Fringe Play, the 1995 Critics' Circle Award and the 1997 Christopher Ewart-Biggs Literary Prize for The Steward of Christendom, and the 1995 Lloyds Private Banking Playwright of the Year Award. Jez Butterworth won the 1995 George Devine Award for Most Promising Playwright, the 1995 Writers' Guild New Writer of the Year Award, the Evening Standard Award for Most Promising Playwright and the 1995 Olivier Award for Best Comedy for Mojo.

The Royal Court was the overall winner of the 1995 Prudential Award for the Arts for creativity, excellence, innovation and accessibility. The Royal Court Theatre Upstairs won the 1995 Peter Brook Empty Space Award for innovation and excellence in theatre.

Michael Wynne won the 1996 Meyer-Whitworth Award for The Knocky. Martin McDonagh won the 1996 George Devine Award, the 1996 Writers' Guild Best Fringe Play Award, the 1996 Critics' Circle Award and the 1996 Evening Standard Award for Most Promising Playwright for The Beauty Queen of Leenane. Marina Carr won the 19th Susan Smith Blackburn Prize (1996/7) for Portia Coughlan. Conor McPherson won the 1997 George Devine Award, the 1997 Critics' Circle Award and the 1997 Evening Standard Award for Most Promising Playwright for The Weir. Ayub Khan-Din won the 1997 Writers' Guild Awards for Best West End Play and Writers' Guild New Writer of the Year and the 1996 John Whiting Award for East is East (co-production with Tamasha).

At the 1998 Tony Awards, Martin McDonagh's The Beauty Queen of Leenane (co-production with Druid Theatre Company) won four awards including Garry Hynes for Best Director and was nominated for a further two. Eugene Ionesco's The Chairs (co-production with Theatre de Complicite) was nominated for six Tony awards. David Hare won the 1998 Time Out Live Award for Outstanding Achievement and six awards in New York including the Drama League, Drama Desk and New York Critics Circle Award for Via Dolorosa. Sarah Kane won the 1998 Arts Foundation Fellowship in Playwriting. Rebecca Prichard won the 1998 Critics' Circle Award for Most Promising Playwright for Yard Gal (co-production with Clean Break).

Conor McPherson won the 1999 Olivier Award for Best New Play for The Weir. The Royal Court won the 1999 ITI Award for Excellence in International Theatre. Sarah Kane's Cleansed was judged Best Foreign Language Play in 1999 by Theater Heute in Germany. Gary Mitchell won the 1999 Pearson Best Play Award for Trust. Rebecca Gilman was joint winner of the 1999 George Devine Award and won the 1999 Evening Standard Award for Most Promising Playwright for The Glory of Living.

Roy Williams and Gary Mitchell were joint winners of the George Devine Award 2000 for Most Promising Playwright for Lift Off and The Force of Change respectively. At the Barclays Theatre Awards 2000 presented by the TMA, Richard Wilson won the Best Director Award for David Gieselmann's Mr Kolpert and Jeremy Herbert won the Best Designer Award for Sarah Kane's 4.48 Psychosis. Gary Mitchell won the Evening Standard's Charles Wintour Award 2000 for Most Promising Playwright for The Force of Change. Stephen Jeffreys' I Just Stopped by to See The Man won an AT&T: On Stage Award 2000. David Eldridge's Under the Blue Sky won the Time Out Live Award 2001 for Best New Play in the West End. Leo Butler won the George Devine Award 2001 for Most Promising Playwright for Redundant. Roy Williams won the Evening Standard's Charles Wintour Award 2001 for Most Promising Playwright for Clubland.

In 1999, the Royal Court won the European theatre prize New Theatrical Realities, presented at Taormina Arte in Sicily, for its efforts in recent years in discovering and producing the work of young British dramatists.

ROYAL COURT BOOKSHOP

The bookshop offers a wide range of playtexts and theatre books, with over 1,000 titles. Located in the downstairs Bar and Food area, the bookshop is open Monday to Saturday, afternoons and evenings.

Many Royal Court playtexts are available for just £2 including works by Harold Pinter, Caryl Churchill, Rebecca Gilman, Martin Crimp, Sarah Kane, Conor McPherson, Ayub Khan-Din, Timberlake Wertenbaker and Roy Williams.

For information on titles and special events, Email: bookshop@royalcourttheatre.com
Tel: 020 7565 5024

FOR THE ROYAL COURT

Royal Court Theatre
Sloane Square, London SW1W 8AS
Tel: 020 7565 5050 Fax: 020 7565 5001
info@royalcourttheatre.com
www.royalcourttheatre.com

ARTISTIC
Artistic Director **Ian Rickson**
Assistant to the Artistic Director **Jo Luke**
Associate Director **Dominic Cooke**
Associate Director International **Elyse Dodgson**
Associate Director Casting **Lisa Makin**
Associate Directors* **Stephen Daldry, James Macdonald, Katie Mitchell, Max Stafford-Clark, Richard Wilson**
Literary Manager **Graham Whybrow**
Literary Associate **Stephen Jeffreys** *
Voice Associate **Patsy Rodenburg***
Casting Assistant **Amy Ball**
International Administrator **Natalie Highwood**
International Associate **Ramin Gray**
Resident Dramatist **Roy Williams**
Writer on Attachment **Chris Dunkley**

YOUNG WRITERS' PROGRAMME
Associate Director **Ola Animashawun**
Education Officer **Christine Hope**
Outreach Worker **Lucy Dunkerley**
Writers Tutor **Simon Stephens***
Administrative Assistant **Lorna Rees**

PRODUCTION
Production Manager **Paul Handley**
Deputy Production Manager **Sue Bird**
Facilities Manager **Fran McElroy**
Production Assistant **Jane Ashfield**
Company Stage Manager **Cath Binks**
Head of Lighting **Johanna Town**
Lighting Deputy **Heidi Riley**
Assistant Electricians **Gavin Owen, Andrew Taylor**
Lighting Board Operator JTD **Richard Wright**
Head of Stage **Martin Riley**
Stage Deputy **Steven Stickler**
Stage Chargehand **Daniel Lockett**
Head of Sound **Paul Arditti**
Sound Deputy **Ian Dickinson**
Sound Operator JTD **Michael Winship** *
Head of Wardrobe **Iona Kenrick**
Wardrobe Deputy **Jackie Orton**

MANAGEMENT
Executive Director **Barbara Matthews**
Assistant to the Executive Director **Nia Janis**
General Manager **Diane Borger**
Administration Interns **Vanessa Cook, Juliette Goodman**
Finance Director **Sarah Preece**
Finance Officer **Rachel Harrison**
Finance Assistant **Martin Wheeler**
Accountant **Simone De Bruyker** *

MARKETING & PRESS
Head of Marketing **Penny Mills**
Head of Press **Ewan Thomson**
Marketing Officer **Charlotte Franklin**
Marketing and Press Assistant **Claire Christou**
Marketing Intern **Jennie Whitell**
Box Office Manager **Neil Grutchfield**
Deputy Box Office Manager **Valli Dakshinamurthi**
Duty Box Office Manager **Glen Bowman**
Box Office Sales Operators **Carol Pritchard, Steven Kuleshnyk**

DEVELOPMENT
Head of Development **Helen Salmon**
Development Associate **Susan Davenport** *
Sponsorship Manager **Rebecca Preston**
Sponsorship Consultant (Maternity cover) **Jeremy Goldstein** *
Development Officer **Alex Lawson**
Development Assistant **Chris James**

FRONT OF HOUSE
Theatre Manager **Elizabeth Brown**
Deputy Theatre Manager **Jeremy Roberts**
Duty House Manager **Suzanne Kean, Paul McLaughlin, Neil Morris***
Bookshop Manager **Peggy Riley**
Assistant Bookshop Manager **Simon David**
Bookshop Assistants **Suzanne Kean, Michael Chance**
Stage Door/Reception **Hannah Caughlin, Simon David, Kelda Holmes, Hannah Lawrence, Tyrone Lucas, Andrew Pepper**
Thanks to all of our ushers

* part-time

First published in English in 2002 by Oberon Books Ltd.
(incorporating Absolute Classics)
521 Caledonian Road, London N7 9RH
Tel: 020 7607 3637 / Fax: 020 7607 3629

e-mail: oberon.books@btinternet.com

A catalogue record for this book is available from the British Library.

ISBN: 1 84002 282 5

Cover design: Oberon Books

Photograph: Gavin Kingcome

Printed in Great Britain by Antony Rowe Ltd, Reading.

Characters

THE YOUNG WOMAN

THE YOUNG MAN

THE FATHER

THE MOTHER

BASTE

Scene 1

Black. Lights up. A living room, a sofa, an armchair and a coffee table a bit to the left down stage. A large window, a bit further back, to the left. To the right of the window, slightly higher up, hangs a clock, showing a quarter to three. A bit beneath the clock, a little to the right, hangs a picture of an infant, a boy. To the left of the window stands an unusually large sideboard. A door in the short wall to the left, a door in the short wall to the right. The YOUNG MAN is lying on the sofa reading a book.

THE YOUNG WOMAN
(*Comes in through the door to the right.*)
I can't stand it
anymore
(*Short pause.*)
No I can't bear it
We can't live like this
(*The YOUNG MAN sits up slowly, closes the book, but marks his page with his index finger.*)
You lay there reading
You don't go out
You don't do anything
(*She makes a list.*)
We haven't got any money
You haven't got any work
We've got
Nothing
(*She goes and sits in the armchair.*)
And you go out less and less
before you used to go to the shop at least
to buy things
went to the post office
You never wanted to go for walks
I've always liked going for walks
Before
yes before I met you
I always went on long walks
Every Sunday I went for a walk
And other days
And I had friends
not so many perhaps

but I had friends
girlfriends
But they
they never come here anymore
Even Marte doesn't come here anymore
She might ring on the doorbell
stand outside talking to me
but she won't come in
Because you just sit there
oozing bad atmosphere
My girlfriends came here a few times
but you just sat here
stiff and awkward
never said a word
(*Laughs resignedly.*)
What an atmosphere
No who could bear that
and so
(*Looks at him.*)
they don't exactly come more often
No-one comes here
(*Short pause.*)
You're not well
You don't like people
Well
(*The YOUNG MAN sighs, looks at her.*)
I can't bear it much longer
(*The YOUNG MAN nods. Pause.*)
And when someone does finally come to visit
it's your parents

THE YOUNG MAN
(*Defends himself.*)
Your parents do occasionally
come here
too
(*Short pause.*)
It's not so long ago
they were here last
And it's not me
who asked my parents to come

THE YOUNG WOMAN
But luckily
they don't stay
very long

THE YOUNG MAN
Yes yes
(*Short pause. He looks at her.*)
And it's not so strange
that they want to see their grandchild
is it
(*A bit angry.*)
Aren't they allowed that
They come here to see their grandchild
Don't you realise
They don't come here
for any other reason

THE YOUNG WOMAN
Yes yes
(*Short pause.*)
And it's about time
they came to see the kid
Wouldn't think
that they cared about him
They could have come before
I mean I really
(*The YOUNG MAN looks down. Pause.*)

THE YOUNG MAN
They don't want to be
any trouble

THE YOUNG WOMAN
Of course I want them to come
Of course
They should just come
(*She looks about the living room, sighs.*)
And I'd better get started with the cleaning
then
before your parents come
It has to be nice and clean

when mother-in-law comes to visit
doesn't it
(*The YOUNG MAN puts his book down on the table, stands up, he walks about the living room a bit.*)
You needn't trouble
(*Loudly.*)
Don't trouble
I can't bear seeing you
pacing up and down
(*Resignedly.*)
I'll do the cleaning and tidying
So don't you worry
yourself
(*The YOUNG MAN goes back to the sofa. Sits down.*)
I'll do everything
You
just relax
Just carry on reading
your book
Just read on
(*She laughs a little.*)
Or if you could perhaps see your way to
going shopping
(*He looks at her somewhat afraid.*)
Or do I have to do that too?
I'll do the shopping
tidy up the flat
cook food for your parents
(*Loudly.*)
No you can go shopping

THE YOUNG MAN
(*Reluctantly.*)
Yes

THE YOUNG WOMAN
(*Surprised, questioningly.*)
Do you dare go out
You don't even dare go to the shop anymore
(*The YOUNG MAN shakes his head. Resignedly.*)
But why did you say yes then

THE YOUNG MAN
Should I have said no

THE YOUNG WOMAN
No you just lie there
just lie there
lie there and read
(*Short pause.*)

THE YOUNG MAN
I can tidy the house

THE YOUNG WOMAN
Good
(*Short pause. Ironic.*)
But aren't you going to write
then
Read
By the way how's it going with your writing
Are you writing anything
Or are you just lying there on the sofa

THE YOUNG MAN
(*Struck by something. Short pause. Ever so slightly enthusiastic.*)
Now I think of it
perhaps I
yes I sent something to a publisher
a while ago

THE YOUNG WOMAN
You sent something to a publisher

THE YOUNG MAN
(*Nods.*)
Yes
(*Short pause.*)
But they probably
don't want it

THE YOUNG WOMAN
It'll be fine
(*The YOUNG MAN nods. Bluntly comforting.*)
I think so
I
You've

(*Short pause.*)
yes as long as I've known you
you've written and written
It'll be several years
soon
Written and written
you have
(*The YOUNG MAN nods.*)
Written and written
(*Abruptly.*)
Shsh
Did you hear something
(*The YOUNG MAN shakes his head.*)
He's not crying
(*The YOUNG MAN shakes his head again.*)
I'll go and have a look
(*The YOUNG WOMAN goes out through the door to the left, and the YOUNG MAN picks up his book, leafs through it, looks for his place, lies on the sofa, carries on leafing through the book, finds his place, starts reading. The YOUNG WOMAN comes back in.*)
No are you reading again
We've got a lot to do
Weren't you going to tidy the flat
(*The YOUNG MAN closes his book, marks his place with his index finger.*)

THE YOUNG MAN
He's sleeping

THE YOUNG WOMAN
Yes
(*Short pause.*)
You don't want to go shopping
(*The YOUNG MAN looks at her despairingly and importunately.*)
You don't dare
No
(*She shakes her head resignedly.*)
No I can't stand this much longer
You never go out
I don't understand you

(Nearly in tears.)
I can't bear this much longer
(The YOUNG MAN sits up, looks about him a little despairingly. The YOUNG WOMAN shakes her head resignedly.)
No
(Pause. The doorbell rings. The YOUNG WOMAN looks at the YOUNG MAN.)
Your parents
Are they here already
There were meant to come later
weren't they
(He looks at her despairingly.)
Do you think
it is your parents
(He just stays sitting, puts his book down on the coffee table.)
Shall I go and open it
(He just sits there, and she goes out through the door to the right. He gets up, goes over to the window, looks out, turns around, looks over to the door on the right where a man of about sixty appears, dressed in a padded jacket. He is carrying a brown shopping bag, looks down, then looks up when he catches sight of the YOUNG MAN, puts the bag in his other hand and then goes towards the YOUNG MAN with outstretched hand and his head bent forward. They meet and shake hands, but don't look at each other.)

THE FATHER
Well hello there hello
Congratulations on the child

THE YOUNG MAN
Thanks
(The YOUNG WOMAN and the MOTHER come in, the MOTHER has a coat on, the YOUNG MAN looks at the MOTHER.)

THE MOTHER
Ah so there you are
there you are
(She stretches out her hand, goes to the YOUNG MAN, who goes towards the MOTHER. They shake hands, she stands with his hand in hers.)

My warmest congratulations
on the baby
(*She looks at the YOUNG WOMAN, lets go of his hand.*)
Well this is nice
This is very nice
At last we shall see our grandchild
I really
(*Looks at the FATHER.*)
I mean we
have been looking forward to this
haven't we

THE FATHER
(*Somewhat hesitatingly.*)
Yes

THE MOTHER
(*With certainty.*)
Yes we have
(*To the YOUNG WOMAN.*)
But where's the baby

YOUNG WOMAN
He's asleep
Lying in the bedroom

THE MOTHER
Aah
But I must have a look at him
right now
(*The YOUNG WOMAN nods. The FATHER looks somewhat despairingly about him, doesn't quite know what to do with himself, he stands there.*)

THE YOUNG MAN
(*To the FATHER.*)
Do sit down

THE FATHER
Yes thanks
(*The FATHER goes and sits in the armchair, puts the bag down beside the chair. The YOUNG WOMAN and the MOTHER go towards the door on the left.*)

THE MOTHER
(*To the FATHER.*)
You can come
too
And look at the little one

THE FATHER
No no
I can wait until he wakes up
(*The MOTHER goes out through the door, and the YOUNG WOMAN goes after her. Pause. To the YOUNG MAN.*)
So this is where you live

THE YOUNG MAN
It is
Yes

THE FATHER
Aha
(*Pause.*)

THE YOUNG MAN
Everything the same
with you

THE FATHER
Everything the same
yes

THE YOUNG MAN
And with them in there
too

THE FATHER
Yes I can't think of anything new
not off hand
anyway

THE YOUNG MAN
There probably isn't anything
then

THE FATHER
Yes
(*Pause.*)
And you're fine

THE YOUNG MAN
Can't complain
Everything's the same

THE FATHER
(*A bit hasty.*)
But have you got any work
(*The YOUNG MAN shakes his head.*)
No no
It's not that easy
to find something to do
I suppose

THE YOUNG MAN
No

THE FATHER
But you get by

THE YOUNG MAN
(*Reluctantly, hesitates.*)
Yes

THE FATHER
(*Looks about him.*)
Nice place to live
anyway
And it's
central
isn't it

THE YOUNG MAN
Oh yes

THE FATHER
But it must be expensive to live here

THE YOUNG MAN
Quite expensive
(*Pause.*)

THE FATHER
But you get by

THE YOUNG MAN
Yes we do
Sort of
(*Laughs a little.*)
anyway

THE FATHER
Yes we took the opportunity
to come into town
your mother and I
Had some errands
to do
And of course we had to
(*Interrupts himself.*)

THE YOUNG MAN
Yes.
I suppose
so
(*A child's crying can be heard.*)

THE FATHER
(*Looks at the YOUNG MAN.*)
He must have woken up

THE YOUNG MAN
Yes
(*Pause.*)
He sleeps nearly all the time

THE FATHER
He doesn't cry very much
(*The YOUNG MAN shakes his head. The crying stops.*)

THE YOUNG MAN
It seems he's quietened down again
(*Short pause.*)
He sleeps a lot
yes

THE FATHER
I see, yes
(*Short pause.*)

No we just thought we'd pop in
you know
since we're in town anyway
yes

THE YOUNG MAN
Yes of course
(*Short pause.*)

THE FATHER
We won't be long
Just thought we'd look in

THE YOUNG MAN
Yes
(*Short pause. The YOUNG WOMAN comes in.*)

THE YOUNG WOMAN
He woke up
a bit
but then he fell asleep again
almost at once
(*The MOTHER comes in.*)

THE MOTHER
(*To the YOUNG WOMAN.*)
No it was silly of me to wake him
I didn't mean to
no it was silly
(*She goes and sits on the sofa.*
To the FATHER.)
You must go and look at him
Such a lovely little boy
You must go and look at him

THE FATHER
Yes
(*The YOUNG WOMAN goes out right.*)

THE MOTHER
(*To the FATHER.*)
But it's not very easy to say
who he looks like
no

But what a lovely little boy
He's nothing like you anyway
(*Then she looks at the YOUNG MAN.*)
Not you either
No he didn't look at all like you
(*Short pause.*)
Nor like me
for that matter
And not
(*Nods towards the door to the right.*)
her
either
(*Quietly, to the YOUNG MAN.*)
But how are things going with you

THE YOUNG MAN
Yes thanks
everything's fine

THE MOTHER
(*Concerned.*)
And the child is well

THE YOUNG MAN
Yes everything is fine

THE MOTHER
But
(*Interrupts herself. Short pause. She looks at the FATHER, the FATHER looks down.*
Pause.)

THE YOUNG MAN
So you took a trip into town

THE MOTHER
Well we had to come and see
the little baby

THE YOUNG MAN
Yes
(*Short pause. To the MOTHER.*)
And then you had a few errands

THE FATHER
Yes

THE MOTHER
(*Quickly.*)
It was mainly to
(*The MOTHER interrupts herself when the YOUNG WOMAN comes in.*)

THE YOUNG WOMAN
I'd better go out
and buy something
for your visit
(*Laughs a little.*)

THE MOTHER/THE FATHER
(*Almost at the same time.*)
No please don't
That's not necessary

THE YOUNG MAN
Yes you caught us a bit unprepared

THE MOTHER
We came a bit early
yes
(*To the YOUNG WOMAN.*)
You must forgive us

THE YOUNG WOMAN
It doesn't matter

THE MOTHER
(*To the YOUNG WOMAN.*)
We just meant to look in
for a moment
We'll go soon
(*To explain.*)
They've changed the bus timetable

THE YOUNG WOMAN
(*To the FATHER.*)
You'd better go and have a look at
him
too

THE FATHER
(Looks down embarrassed, hesitates.)
Yes

THE YOUNG WOMAN
You two
(Looks at the YOUNG MAN, then at the FATHER.)
can go and look at him

THE FATHER
Or
we could wait

THE YOUNG WOMAN
No go and look at him

THE YOUNG MAN
(Gets up.)
Well come on then
(The FATHER gets up, and the YOUNG MAN and the FATHER go out through the door to the left. Pause.)

THE YOUNG WOMAN
But I'd better
go off shopping for a bit
so we've got something to give you
I was just on my way out the door
when you arrived

THE MOTHER
(Quickly.)
No it's not necessary
We have to go soon anyway
Our bus goes soon
you see
(Short pause.)
We were just popping by
for a moment

THE YOUNG WOMAN
Yes

THE MOTHER
We had to have a look
at the little one

since we were
in town
(*Looks at her.*)
But my goodness he's lovely

THE YOUNG WOMAN
Yes

THE MOTHER
Yes a really lovely child
You've been lucky
(*Short pause.*)
And everything's alright
both with you and the child

THE YOUNG WOMAN
Nothing out of the ordinary
everything has gone as it should
Everything is fine

THE MOTHER
Well that's good
(*Pause.*)
And you've got maternity leave from work

THE YOUNG WOMAN
Yes

THE MOTHER
Well that's nice
isn't it
that you get a little time
to take care of the child
(*Pause.*)
And we've brought a little present
(*Laughs a little.*)
Should think so too
(*She goes to the shopping bag, lifts it up, puts it on the armchair, opens the zip, takes out a packet, stands with the packet in her hand.*)
It's not very much
just a little thing
We so wanted to get something for the child
(*She passes the present to the YOUNG WOMAN.*)

THE YOUNG WOMAN
(*Takes it.*)
Thanks very much
It's kind of you

THE MOTHER
It's not very much
(*The YOUNG WOMAN is left standing fiddling with the wrapping, doesn't really know what she should do. Short pause.*)
Yes he's a lovely baby
(*The MOTHER shakes her head resignedly. The FATHER comes in through the door. Tense, to the FATHER.*)
What do you think

THE FATHER
(*Sincerely with emphasis behind his words.*)
Yes he's a lovely boy
(*The MOTHER looks meaningfully at the YOUNG WOMAN, the YOUNG MAN comes in, he sees that the YOUNG WOMAN stands fumbling with the packet. Short pause.*)

THE YOUNG MAN
(*To the YOUNG WOMAN.*)
We've been given a present
(*She nods.*)
Better get on and open it then
(*To the MOTHER and FATHER.*)
Thank you very much
(*The YOUNG WOMAN sits on the sofa, starts opening the packet.*)

THE MOTHER
(*Apologetically.*)
It's not very much
just a little thing

THE YOUNG WOMAN
(*Opens the packet, takes out a blue blanket, holds it up before her, and then for the YOUNG MAN to see.*)
How nice

THE YOUNG MAN
(*Nods.*)
Yes

THE MOTHER
It's so difficult to know what to buy
It's just a little thing
(*The YOUNG WOMAN puts down the blanket on the coffee table, stands up, takes the wrapper with her and goes out through the door to the right. The MOTHER picks up the blanket, looks at it. To the FATHER.*)
Well isn't he lovely

THE FATHER
(*Smiles to himself a little.*)
Oh yes
(*Short pause.*)
But who does he resemble

THE MOTHER
You tell me
(*She folds the blanket neatly, puts it back on the coffee table.*)

THE FATHER
No I can't say

THE MOTHER
Not you
at any rate

THE FATHER
No

THE MOTHER
Perhaps
(*Interrupts herself.*)
No I don't know
(*The FATHER goes and sits on the sofa.*
To the YOUNG MAN.)
Yes you've got a fine son there
(*The YOUNG WOMAN comes in. She has put on a jacket.*)

THE MOTHER
(*To the YOUNG WOMAN, quickly.*)
No don't trouble yourself
We're going in a minute
It just turned out that way today

They've changed the bus timetable
(*She looks at the FATHER.*)
Haven't they

THE FATHER
(*Pulls up the sleeve of his coat, looks at his watch.*)
Yes we'd better be going soon
(*Looks at the MOTHER.*)
It's nearly time

THE MOTHER
(*Looks at the YOUNG WOMAN in explanation.*)
We just wanted to visit
the little one

THE FATHER
It's just a short visit
(*The FATHER gets up, picks up his bag, lifts it up onto the armchair, pulls up the zip, walks across the room.*)

THE MOTHER
(*Gets up, she too walks across the room.*)
Yes we can stay longer
some other time
But today we'll have to make do

THE FATHER
(*To the YOUNG MAN.*)
Yes you know
there aren't many buses
running
these days

THE MOTHER
(*To the YOUNG WOMAN.*)
To tell the truth
it's
the last bus
for the day

THE YOUNG MAN
(*Questioningly.*)
Have they cut out
the other buses

THE FATHER
Yes
(*Short pause.*
To the YOUNG MAN.)
But you can come and look in to us some time
all three of you

THE MOTHER
(*In assent.*)
Yes you really must
This summer
when it's warm and light
then you really must
come and visit us
mustn't they

THE YOUNG MAN
Well thanks for looking in
(*Short pause.*)
You'll have to come for
a longer visit
next time
(*The MOTHER and FATHER go towards the door.*)
I can see you out
(*The MOTHER and FATHER go out through the door, stop, look at the YOUNG WOMAN.*)

THE MOTHER
Yes it's been very short
But that's what happens
when you don't have the sense to check the bus times
Well look after yourself

THE FATHER
Yes
look after yourself
(*The MOTHER and FATHER go out through the door to the right. The YOUNG MAN goes after them, the YOUNG WOMAN goes and sits in the armchair, opens her legs wide, looks somewhat forlorn. Pause. The YOUNG MAN comes in again. The YOUNG WOMAN gets up, walks across the room, the YOUNG MAN goes and sits in the armchair.*)

THE YOUNG WOMAN
(*To the YOUNG MAN.*)
There you see
No-one wants to be here
Not even your parents
They'd hardly arrived
before they were
off again
Just took a quick look at the child
Talked a bit about who he looked like
and then they just left
(*Short pause.*)
They hardly seemed to think
you were the father
(*She laughs a bit. The YOUNG MAN gets up, lies down on the sofa. Pause.*)
I don't even think
they liked him

THE YOUNG MAN
(*Irritated.*)
Of course they did

THE YOUNG WOMAN
I'm not so sure

THE YOUNG MAN
Yes of course they did
Why do you say that

THE YOUNG WOMAN
Maybe they did like him

THE YOUNG MAN
They liked him
obviously
They liked him very much

THE YOUNG WOMAN
Alright they did then
(*Pause.*)
But I'd better go shopping
so we have something to eat

(*Questioningly.*)
Right then
(*Resolutely.*)
And if he cries
you must pick him up
(*The YOUNG MAN nods and while the YOUNG WOMAN stands and looks at him he picks up his book from the coffee table, and starts looking for his place, finds it, starts reading.*)
Right I'll be off then
(*He nods without looking at her. She goes out through the door to the right, he lays the book before him on his chest, and lays there looking straight ahead. Pause. Light down. Black.*)

Scene 2

Black. Lights up. Dusk outside the window. The clock on the wall shows about half past five. The YOUNG MAN is still lying on the sofa, with the book on his chest. He gets up, goes over to the window, looks out. The YOUNG WOMAN comes in through the door to the right, with her jacket on, she has a plastic bag in her hand.

THE YOUNG WOMAN
(*Hands out letter to the YOUNG MAN.*)
Letter for you

THE YOUNG MAN
(*Turns slowly towards her.*
A bit scared.)
Letter

THE YOUNG WOMAN
Yes from a publisher
(*She goes over to him, hands him the letter, stands there and looks at the letter.*)
Aren't you curious
(*He shakes his head.*)

THE YOUNG MAN
Yes actually
a bit

THE YOUNG WOMAN
Yes perhaps
(*Interrupts herself.*)

THE YOUNG MAN
(*Quickly.*)
But you were gone so long

THE YOUNG WOMAN
Yes
(*Short pause.*)
I dropped in on Marte
(*Short pause.*)
She's coming round by the way
(*She laughs a bit.*)
What a day
First your parents come
And now maybe Marte
We haven't had this many visits
for as long as I can remember
(*Short pause.*)
But your parents didn't stay so long of course
(*Quickly.*)
Did he sleep

THE YOUNG MAN
Yes

THE YOUNG WOMAN
Then he won't
sleep tonight anyway
Has he been asleep the whole time

THE YOUNG MAN
(*Nods.*)
Yes
I haven't heard a thing from him

THE YOUNG WOMAN
Haven't you been in
and looked at him

THE YOUNG MAN
Yes a couple of times

THE YOUNG WOMAN
Well now it's about time he woke up
But em
(*Short pause.*)

Marte and I thought we'd go out for a bit
this evening

THE YOUNG MAN
(*Questioningly.*)
Yes

THE YOUNG WOMAN
That's alright isn't it
(*He doesn't reply.*
Quickly.)
I can't just sit indoors
you know
Well
She's coming very soon
and then we'll go
out for a bit
(*She lifts up the carrier bag.*)
I've bought some food
You can eat
if you like
(*She laughs.*)
I can't be bothered to cook dinner
I had a bit of food at Marte's

THE YOUNG MAN
Marte's coming here

THE YOUNG WOMAN
Yes but only to the door of course
(*Short pause.*)
She doesn't of course want to be here
with the atmosphere you
spread around you
(*She laughs briefly.*)

THE YOUNG MAN
(*Can't be bothered.*)
Yes yes
(*Short pause.*)
You went over to Marte's

THE YOUNG WOMAN
Yes

(*Short pause.*)
But now you must open your letter

THE YOUNG MAN
No not yet

THE YOUNG WOMAN
Why not

THE YOUNG MAN
(*Hesitates.*)
No

THE YOUNG WOMAN
I'd better go and wake him up
He can't sleep
all the time
can he
No he can't sleep any more now
I'd better wake him
Or you maybe you can
wake him up
change his nappy
give him some food

THE YOUNG MAN
(*Nods.*)
Yes alright
(*Short pause.*)
What time is Marte coming

THE YOUNG WOMAN
She's coming now
straight away
I'll just go and get ready
(*He stays standing looking down and to the side.*)
But you understand
don't you
that if you want to sit indoors
all day
and don't want to go out
then I'll have to
I can't sit indoors all the time

You hardly open your mouth
you just lie there
lie there on the sofa reading
(*Resignedly.*)
Yes

THE YOUNG MAN
Yes I know

THE YOUNG WOMAN
In the past Marte and I were often together
she'd come round all day
we'd sit there
talking and laughing
having a nice time
But since you and I started living together
it just doesn't work
It doesn't work

THE YOUNG MAN
Yes I know
(*Pause.*)

THE YOUNG WOMAN
But now you must open your letter
(*The YOUNG MAN opens the letter, runs his eye across it. Questioningly.*)
Didn't they want
what you've written
(*He nods.*)
But this time you thought it would be alright
Didn't you

THE YOUNG MAN
Yes I suppose I did

THE YOUNG WOMAN
But how long are you going to carry on
with this writing then
You can't just sit there writing
year in
year out
You can't just
(*Interrupts herself. Pause.*)

Maybe you're not really meant to be a writer
Yes I mean it
Either you have to get something published
or
you'll have to find something else
to do
You can't just sit indoors
and never go out
and write things that no-one cares about

THE YOUNG MAN
No
(*He sets down the letter on the window sill, goes and sits in the armchair. Pause.*)

THE YOUNG WOMAN
So you don't want to go in to the baby then
(*Short pause. She goes and sets down her bag in front of him on the coffee table.*)
Here's your food
at any rate
(*She goes out through the door to the left. Short pause, then she comes in again, she carries a mirror, make-up, a blouse.*)
No he's sleeping so nicely I'll leave him be
You'll have to change him when he wakes up
(*She goes over to the coffee table, puts down the mirror, make-up and blouse on the coffee table. She points to the plastic bag.*)
Can't you carry those things out to the kitchen
(*He nods, gets up, takes the bag and goes out to the right. She takes off her jacket, puts it over the arm of the armchair, and pulls her jumper over her head and stands there in just her bra, she sits in the sofa, takes a few bits of make-up, starts applying it. The YOUNG MAN comes in, sits on the sofa.*)

THE YOUNG MAN
Will it be long before Marte comes

THE YOUNG WOMAN
No she was going to come straight away
She's coming soon
(*He nods.*)
But your parents
They really are

(*She interrupts herself, shakes her head while applying her make-up.*)
Imagine coming like that
and then going at once
I'm sure they
didn't like the kid
(*Short pause.*)
It's probably because they don't like me
that they don't like the child
They've never liked me
Your father could hardly be bothered to look at the kid

THE YOUNG MAN
It's not like that

THE YOUNG WOMAN
Isn't it
How is it then
Your father could hardly be bothered
to go and look at the kid

THE YOUNG MAN
He's just embarrassed
he didn't want to be any trouble

THE YOUNG WOMAN
Just like you
(*She has put on strong red lipstick. She gets up, walks around the room, with the mirror in her hand, pouting her lips, puts on even more lipstick. She turns to him, pouting.*)
Is this alright

THE YOUNG MAN
Yes fine

THE YOUNG WOMAN
(*As if lost in her own thoughts.*)
It really is too bad about this publisher
that they don't want to publish
what you've written
(*She picks up the blouse from the coffee table, puts it on. She walks around the room, looks at herself in the mirror again, puts on a bit more lipstick. She goes over to the window, stands*

there looking out, sticks out her bottom somewhat. The YOUNG MAN sits looking at her. She turns towards the YOUNG MAN.)
Here comes Marte
I can see her down on the street
I think I'll just go down
and save you
(*Laughs briefly.*)
having to see her
(*She goes and picks up her jacket from the arm of the chair, puts it on, picks up her jumper from the floor, takes it, the mirror and the make-up things and goes and puts it all in the window, the she goes towards the door to the right. She stops.*)
I'll
be off
then

THE YOUNG MAN
What time are you coming home

THE YOUNG WOMAN
I won't be very late
Don't you
wait up for me
you just
go to bed

THE YOUNG MAN
Em

THE YOUNG WOMAN
Was there something

THE YOUNG MAN
My parents phoned

THE YOUNG WOMAN
(*As if surprised.*)
No really, did they
(*As if interested.*)
Was it anything in particular

THE YOUNG MAN
No
They just phoned

And then Mum said
that she'd been so excited
to see her grandchild
she said
(*He laughs a little.*)
that she had forgotten to give us a present
she had brought for the baby
Apparently it was a little toy

THE YOUNG WOMAN
That was very kind
to bring a present for him
anyway
(*She picks up the blanket from the coffee table, stands looking at it.*)

THE YOUNG MAN
She'd send the toy
She said
(*Short pause.*)

THE YOUNG WOMAN
(*For something to say.*)
It's not often your parents phone
(*Pause. She pulls out a drawer in the sideboard, puts in the blanket, pushes in the drawer.*)

THE YOUNG MAN
And then they said
that they'd arrived home safely
(*The doorbell rings.*)

THE YOUNG WOMAN
It's probably Marte

THE YOUNG MAN
(*Apologetically.*)
I just thought I'd tell you

THE YOUNG WOMAN
I'll
be off
then

(*The YOUNG MAN nods, and the YOUNG WOMAN goes out through the door to the right. From the kitchen.*)
There are some clean bottles and teats
on the draining board
(*He gets up, goes over to the window, stands looking out through the window, then he picks up the letter, stands looking at it, puts it back in the window, then goes over to the sofa, lies down, picks up his book, leafs forwards, finds his place, reads a little, puts the book down on the coffee table, gets up, goes over to the window again, stands there, looks out. He picks up the jumper, stands fiddling with it. Lights fade, black.*)

Scene 3

Black. Lights up. Outside the window it is dark. The clock stands at half past two. On the coffee table is a child's bottle with a little milk in. The YOUNG MAN is lying on the sofa and staring straight ahead, he gets up and goes to the window, looks out into the darkness. The baby starts crying, he goes over to an old perambulator which stands by the window with the hood up, starts rolling it to and fro, stops, then stands rocking it up and down. The child's crying abates. He goes and sits on the sofa, but gets up, goes over to the window, fetches the letter and returns to the sofa, and sits looking at the letter. He puts the letter down on the coffee table, gets up, goes over to the window, looks out, and remains standing with his gaze turned out through the window. He goes and lies down on the sofa. The YOUNG WOMAN comes in through the door to the right, with her jacket on, a bit excited. He looks at her.

THE YOUNG WOMAN
(*A bit surprised.*)
You're up
I thought
(*She looks at the pram.*)
Is he awake

THE YOUNG MAN
No

THE YOUNG WOMAN
No

THE YOUNG MAN
He's been asleep for a while
now
But he has been awake several times
Almost impossible to get him to sleep
He falls asleep
wakes up again
carried on like that the whole time

THE YOUNG WOMAN
(*Questioningly.*)
He's in the pram

THE YOUNG MAN
(*A little irritated.*)
There's no point
trying to get him to be quiet in his bed
He wakes up all the time
and if he's lying in his bed
its impossible to get him to fall asleep again
I had to rock him
push him to and fro
to get him to sleep

THE YOUNG WOMAN
Didn't his dummy help
either

THE YOUNG MAN
No

THE YOUNG WOMAN
(*Goes over to the pram, peeps down into it. To the YOUNG MAN.*)
But he's asleep now
nice and safe
(*Questioningly.*)
He's just been crying
(*Short pause.*)
You've changed his nappy

THE YOUNG MAN
Yes
Twice
(*Pause.*)

THE YOUNG WOMAN
And you've fed him

THE YOUNG MAN
Yes
(*Short pause.*)

THE YOUNG WOMAN
I didn't expect that you'd
be up
It got rather late
(*Laughs briefly.*)
You're sitting waiting for me

THE YOUNG MAN
Yes
No
He woke up didn't he
so I had to get up
He woke up all the time
so it was just as well to get up
and go into the living room

THE YOUNG WOMAN
So you had gone to bed

THE YOUNG MAN
(*Lies.*)
Yes
(*Pause. He sits up in the sofa.*)
Have you had a nice time

THE YOUNG WOMAN
I have yes

THE YOUNG MAN
You met
your girlfriend
I mean em

THE YOUNG WOMAN
Yes
Marte yes

THE YOUNG MAN
(*Somewhat despairing.*)
But you're so late

THE YOUNG WOMAN
You've waited up

THE YOUNG MAN
(*Nods, hesitates, reluctantly.*)
Yes
(*Overcomes his resistance.*)
But where have you been

THE YOUNG WOMAN
(*A little resignedly.*)
Right
(*She starts walking to and fro.*)
No don't start
this again

THE YOUNG MAN
But you can tell me
where you've been
can't you

THE YOUNG WOMAN
(*Suddenly looks a bit tired, pulls up the sleeve of her jacket to look at her watch.*)
Can't we just go to bed
It's late
I want to go to bed
I can tell you tomorrow
instead
(*The YOUNG MAN doesn't answer. He lies on the sofa again. The YOUNG WOMAN goes over to the window again and stands looking out. Pause.*)

THE YOUNG MAN
(*With his gaze right ahead.*)
You just
go to bed then

THE YOUNG WOMAN
(*Turns towards him.*)
But don't you want to go to bed yourself
(*Pause.*)

THE YOUNG MAN
I don't think I can sleep
I'm tired
but I'm not going to be able to sleep

THE YOUNG WOMAN
I'm sure you can
if you just try

THE YOUNG MAN
Yes

THE YOUNG WOMAN
I'm tired at any rate

THE YOUNG MAN
But that car
I saw
I was there looking to see
if you were coming
I mean
Who was it drove you home
I don't mean
Don't misunderstand me
But
Well

THE YOUNG WOMAN
(*Resignedly.*)
That's tonight ruined
I'm going to have some wine
(*She goes out through the door to the right, comes back with a bottle of wine in one hand and a half full glass of wine in the other. Looks at him.*)
So
I'm ready now
Ask away

THE YOUNG MAN
No I'm not going to ask anything

THE YOUNG WOMAN
I'm just a bit tired
(*She drinks wine.*)

THE YOUNG MAN
Yes

THE YOUNG WOMAN
Nothing in particular
has happened
just so that you know
But what is it
you want to know
(*Makes a list.*)
Where have you been
Who have you been with
and so on

THE YOUNG MAN
You can tell me
something
at least

THE YOUNG WOMAN
(*Resignedly.*)
I suppose so
(*Drinks wine.*)

THE YOUNG MAN:
No you don't have to
(*Short pause.*)
I just get so worried
I don't know

THE YOUNG WOMAN
Yes
(*Short pause. Makes a list.*)
Well I met my girlfriend
Marte
yeah
And then we had dinner
in a restaurant
And then we went

to a bar
And then
oh yes we went to a night club
(*The YOUNG MAN sits up on the sofa, looks at the YOUNG WOMAN.*)
Was there anything else
you wanted to know
No
(*Short pause.*)
Can we go to bed now
I'm tired
I want to sleep
(*She looks at her glass.*)
I'll just finish this
(*Short pause.*)
And then we can go to bed
Can't we

THE YOUNG MAN
(*Looks at her.*)
Can't you
come over here
sit here a bit
talk to me a bit
I'm not going to be able to sleep
I can tell
Can't we talk a little

THE YOUNG WOMAN
Talk
You?

THE YOUNG MAN
Yes
I've waited so long
You don't have to go to bed
Straight away

THE YOUNG WOMAN
(*Sighs.*)
But I'm so tired
And

(*Looks at him.*)
a little drunk too perhaps
If I drink any more now
then I'm certainly going to get drunk at any rate
(*She drinks a little wine, goes over to the sofa, puts the wine bottle and the glass on the floor, picks up the letter that's lying on the coffee table, sits down, looks at the letter. Looks at him. Ironic.*)
You're going to have a book published
soon
Let's drink to that
(*She puts down the letter, pours more wine into her glass, raises it to him, but he shakes his head.*)
Now you're not going to just sit here writing and writing
you're going to get something published
as well
Ha
Not bad
(*He shakes his head.*)

THE YOUNG MAN
Can't you stop that now

THE YOUNG WOMAN
(*Puts her glass on the floor, picks up the letter again, reads, grins a little to herself, looks at him, questioningly.*)
They didn't want it?
'Doesn't satisfy our high standards of quality'

THE YOUNG MAN
(*Laughs a bit.*)
Give it here
(*She passes him the letter, which he tears up, lengthways and across, screws up the paper. She stays sitting there as if she is bored. Then she looks at him.*)
They didn't want it
no
Nice response
I laboured and laboured
over that
For at least a year

THE YOUNG WOMAN
Longer surely

THE YOUNG MAN
Well
a long time anyway
I've been
working on that

THE YOUNG WOMAN
But there are many publishers
(*She lifts her glass, drinks a little.*)
No this is going to end up with drunkenness

THE YOUNG MAN
(*Questioningly.*)
You've drunk a lot
(*She nods.*)
But you seem quite sober

THE YOUNG WOMAN
I haven't drunk
that much
But now I fancy
a bit of wine
(*She drinks a little more. Short pause.*)
Have you done anything
then

THE YOUNG MAN
No
I just sat here
Walked around
with the pram
(*She laughs briefly.*)
Waited for you
(*He looks at her, laughs.*)
But where have you been
Can't you tell me something
(*Questioningly.*)
You were with that girl Marte

THE YOUNG WOMAN
(*Nods, a little scared.*)
Yes

THE YOUNG MAN
Well then
(*He gets a bit worried, looks at her.*)
No it's ridiculous

THE YOUNG WOMAN
Why

THE YOUNG MAN
No I can't
It's so silly

THE YOUNG WOMAN
Say

THE YOUNG MAN
No
I can't

THE YOUNG WOMAN
Why not?

THE YOUNG MAN
(*Looks at the YOUNG WOMAN, sententiously.*)
You haven't been with Marte

THE YOUNG WOMAN
(*Drinks a little wine.*)
Haven't I
You've
(*Interrupts herself.*)

THE YOUNG MAN
And neither of us thought you were
either

THE YOUNG WOMAN
No
Alright
If you say so

THE YOUNG MAN
Marte says hello by the way
(*Resignedly.*)
Don't lie
Why must you lie
(*The YOUNG WOMAN looks down. Pause.*)
So you haven't been with Marte
She phoned you you see
A little while after you'd gone out
(*Pause.*)

THE YOUNG WOMAN
No alright
I haven't
then
(*She drinks a little wine.*)
Shall we row
is that what you want
Can't we go to bed
instead
We can talk
tomorrow
(*The YOUNG WOMAN sits next to him, puts an arm around his shoulders. They sit for a while, he is staring straight ahead, she shakes his shoulder a little.*)
Can't we go to bed instead
eh
Can't we
I can tell you tomorrow
(*He just sits there, staring straight ahead, sitting fiddling with the paper.*)
Come on
let's go to bed
(*She pulls him to her.*)
Hm
Come on now
Can't we
We can talk tomorrow
I can tell you tomorrow

THE YOUNG MAN
But you can tell me where you've been
at least
You haven't been with Marte at any rate

THE YOUNG WOMAN
(*Looks at him.*)
Yes I have
You're just lying
She can't have phoned
because she's actually
been with me
I know you
Your tricks
Why do you bother
I know you
so well
(*She sighs.*)

THE YOUNG MAN
But that car
Who was it drove you home

THE YOUNG WOMAN
(*Resignedly.*)
Okay, okay
(*Short pause.*)
As you like
(*Short pause. She pulls away her arm.*)
We could just sit here gawping
as we always do
every single evening
Perhaps we could watch tv
too
even though it is the middle of the night

THE YOUNG MAN
No
you just go to bed
(*Looks at her.*)
I mean it

THE YOUNG WOMAN
(*Gets up, a bit upset.*)
You never go out do you
You never want anything
just sit here
Doing your writing
(*Resignedly.*)
Yes
(*Short pause.*)
No-one comes here
No-one wants to visit us
here
And then your parents
Came here today
and left almost before they'd arrived
(*She sighs.*)

THE YOUNG MAN
Yes I know
I know all of it
(*Pause. Looks at her.*)
But
But we're good
together
too
surely
aren't we

THE YOUNG WOMAN
Yes yes
It's not that

THE YOUNG MAN
And it was you
that was so keen
that we should have children

THE YOUNG WOMAN
Don't start all that as well
It's a wonder you don't
get sick of yourself
that you don't

bore yourself to death
You've said all this
often enough
Haven't you got anything new
to say
(*She goes to the door to the left, stops, looks at him.*)
No I'm going to bed
(*Short pause.*)
You don't want anything
do you
You don't even want to
go outside the door
not even to the shop
You just sit indoors
to like, do your writing
I can't just sit indoors
I can't bear it
It drives me mad

THE YOUNG MAN
Can't you even tell me
(*Throws the screwed up paper across the floor.*)
who drove you home

THE YOUNG WOMAN
Just lay off will you
Don't start
I'm tired
Can't we go to bed
It's late
(*Looks at the clock on the wall.*)
Is that the time
(*Laughs briefly.*)
I didn't know it was that late
(*Looks at the young man friendlily.*)
Come on
Let's go to bed
Can't we
He'll wake up soon
(*Looks at the pram.*)
that feller

Just a couple of hours left
(*Laughs a little.*)
and he'll be in full swing
(*The YOUNG WOMAN goes over to the sofa, stretches her hand out to the YOUNG MAN.*)
Come
Let's go to bed
You can lie close to me
Come on now
Can't we
We can lie close to each other and sleep
Come on
(*The YOUNG MAN stays sitting. She pulls back her hand. Pause. She sighs.*)
That's tonight ruined
(*She sits once again next to him on the sofa, picks up her glass, drinks a little wine. Pause. She looks at him.*)
Hey
Can't we go to bed
We can lay close to each other
Comfort one another

THE YOUNG MAN
(*Gets up.*)
But I've waited so long
You could have come home a little earlier
I sit here waiting and waiting
Go over to the window
Go back to the sofa
Lie down
Get up again
Waiting and waiting

THE YOUNG WOMAN
You mustn't wait like that
(*Short pause.*)
There's no point to it
It would be better to go out
even for you
now and again
At any rate

You can't just sit indoors
In any case I can't bear to
sit indoors all the time
You never go out
Not in the day
Not in the evening
Not even for a walk
You never want to go for a walk
not even with me and the baby
You're always indoors

THE YOUNG MAN
Yes yes

THE YOUNG WOMAN
I can't sit indoors
all the time just because you do
(*Pause.*)
I'm not like that
Something has to happen
I have to see people

THE YOUNG MAN
Yes

THE YOUNG WOMAN
And if only it was possible
for people to come here
But that doesn't work
either
Because then you just go and hide
As soon as someone steps inside the door
you go off
into the bedroom
It's no good
I can't go out
and meet people
And they can't
come here
Because if someone comes here
and you don't
go off into the bedroom
but sit in here
then you are so stiff

and so strange
that the atmosphere
gets so stiff
it's unbearable
(*Nearly screams.*)
Even your parents left
almost before they'd arrived
(*Short pause.*)
Everything gets so stiff and disgusting
It's no good
I can't bear people coming here

THE YOUNG MAN
No

THE YOUNG WOMAN
You're afraid of people aren't you
You can't live like that

THE YOUNG MAN
(*Sits in the armchair.*)
But you came back so late
You said you'd be home early

THE YOUNG WOMAN
(*Irritated.*)
Alright alright

THE YOUNG MAN
(*Conciliatory.*)
But you had
a nice time

THE YOUNG WOMAN
(*Bluntly.*)
Yes we had
a nice time
yes

THE YOUNG MAN
And the hours passed by

THE YOUNG WOMAN
Yes
And now the rest
of the night

will pass
as well

THE YOUNG MAN
You don't want to say anything
to tell me anything
Not even
where you've been

THE YOUNG WOMAN
I do
But I'm tired

THE YOUNG MAN
(*Forces it out.*)
Have you

THE YOUNG WOMAN
(*Interrupts him.*)
Yes I have danced with a lot of men
if it was that
you were going to say
Talked
Had a nice time
Yes I have
I have met a few of my friends
from work
I have to meet them sometimes
now I'm on maternity leave
I met Jan* and a few others
I can't just sit indoors
even if you do
You just sit there
don't you
Yes

THE YOUNG MAN
But it's really good
between us
isn't it

* pronounced Yahn

THE YOUNG WOMAN
(*Resignedly.*)
Yes yes
(*Short pause.*)
Yes it is really good
it is
I know that
It is really good

THE YOUNG MAN
And we've stayed together
quite a long time
We don't have
such a bad time

THE YOUNG WOMAN
No
(*Short pause.*)
But we were so young
We met at school
And then
Well
I have to meet other people besides you
You weren't like this before
you just get worse and worse
I can't sit indoors
all the time
even if you want to
Well
(*Short pause.*)
And if you can't

THE YOUNG MAN
(*Suggests.*)
Start studying or something
(*Questioningly.*)
Is that what you were going to say

THE YOUNG WOMAN
Yes
You have to think of
something or other

Get yourself a job
or something

THE YOUNG MAN
Get your hair cut and get a job
Is that what you wanted to say
(*Laughs briefly.*)

THE YOUNG WOMAN
Oh very funny
(*Short pause.*)
But even you could earn
a little money
Yes I mean it
And this publisher didn't want
your manuscript did he
You can't just
sit indoors writing
either
year in year out
Either you have to get something published
or you'll just have to
find something else
to do
(*He looks down. A bit comfortingly.*)
But it often happens
that people can't get what they write published
That's how it usually is
isn't it
Everyone gets rejected
don't they
(*He nods.*)
It's not all that easy
to get something published
is it
(*He shrugs his shoulders. She looks comfortingly at him.*)
Don't take it so hard
Don't let it get you down
Maybe you weren't meant
to write
for that matter

THE YOUNG MAN
No

THE YOUNG WOMAN
It could well be
that you were meant to do something else entirely

THE YOUNG MAN
Perhaps
(*Short pause.*)
But I can't concentrate
because of him over there
(*Points to the pram.*)
screaming all day long

THE YOUNG WOMAN
It was going better
before he was born
you mean

THE YOUNG MAN
Maybe not

THE YOUNG WOMAN
One rejection doesn't matter all that much
It's not all that important
Is it

THE YOUNG MAN
I've got at least ten

THE YOUNG WOMAN
(*Looks at him surprised.*)
No
it's not that many
is it

THE YOUNG MAN
Yes
(*He laughs. The YOUNG WOMAN pours wine into her glass, gets up, walks over to the window, stands as if in her own thoughts, a little dreamily, looks out, then takes off her jacket, remains standing there with it under her arm.*)
Yes

I must have ten
at least
I just haven't
told you
I've received the letters
then thrown them away

THE YOUNG WOMAN
(*Not really following.*)
Yeah

THE YOUNG MAN
(*Gets up, walks about the room a little.*)
I just haven't told you
I've fetched the post
and each time
I've just thrown it
(*Interrupts himself.*)

THE YOUNG WOMAN
(*Staring straight ahead.*)
Shall we go to bed

THE YOUNG MAN
I have been rejected
by one publisher after another
(*Looks at her.*)
Can't you listen

THE YOUNG WOMAN
I'm listening
I'm tired

THE YOUNG MAN
You're not listening
You're just standing there
looking out
What are you looking for
The man who drove you home
perhaps
Can't you tell me who it was
that drove you home
Who was it

THE YOUNG WOMAN
(*Sharply.*)
Drove me home

THE YOUNG MAN
Yes

THE YOUNG WOMAN
I took a taxi
(*The YOUNG MAN stands staring at the floor in front of him. The YOUNG WOMAN turns and looks at him.*)
Yes
I did

THE YOUNG MAN
Don't lie
I saw it
(*Despairingly. He looks at her.*)
That wasn't a taxi
I saw when you arrived

THE YOUNG WOMAN
(*Walks about the room a bit.*)
Alright I got a lift then
But I can't tell you
that Baste* drove me home
Because if I did
you'd just start making
such a hell of a fuss
And that would be tonight ruined
So
Baste drove me home
Now you know

THE YOUNG MAN
But if you met him
out then
he must have been drinking
Baste I mean

* pronounced Bus-tah

THE YOUNG WOMAN
No he wasn't drinking, just imagine

THE YOUNG MAN
Why were you sitting such a long time
down there in his car

THE YOUNG WOMAN
I didn't sit for a long time
in his car
Now lay off

THE YOUNG MAN
Alright then

THE YOUNG WOMAN
We just talked a bit
(*The child moans, and the YOUNG WOMAN goes over and starts to push the pram, stands still, pushing the pram up and down. The child quietens down. To the YOUNG MAN.*)
I want to go to bed
I'm tired
(*She goes over to the window, stands looking out.*)

THE YOUNG MAN
Why do you stand there dreaming

THE YOUNG WOMAN
I'm not dreaming

THE YOUNG MAN
Alright then

THE YOUNG WOMAN
(*Turns to the YOUNG MAN.*)
I have to be allowed to meet other people
besides you

THE YOUNG MAN
And go home
with your male work colleague
of an evening
at night
(*Ironic.*)
when you are on maternity leave

THE YOUNG WOMAN
No

THE YOUNG MAN
I know it
I know you've been
with him
and not with that
girlfriend of yours
That's just
something you say
That much I understand at least

THE YOUNG WOMAN
Alright.
(*Looks hard at him.*)
Yes I have then
I have
I've been
with Baste
all evening
Been to his house
Was there anything else
you wanted to know
Yes
(*The YOUNG MAN collapses a little.*)
We drove around in his car
listened to music
and we talked
Yes we did
And we've been round at his house
Him and me
Just us two
Are you satisfied
now

THE YOUNG MAN
(*A little surprised.*)
Have you

THE YOUNG WOMAN
(*Laughs a little.*)
No
I'm only joking

THE YOUNG MAN
(Relieved.)
It's not true

THE YOUNG WOMAN
I've been
with Marte
It's true
And you won't get me to believe
that she phoned you

THE YOUNG MAN
But
I saw didn't I
(Short pause.)
You know, that car

THE YOUNG WOMAN
Yes
I've told you what that was

THE YOUNG MAN
You weren't joking

THE YOUNG WOMAN
It was just Marte's boyfriend
He picked her up
and gave me a lift home
too
Alright
Can we go to bed now

THE YOUNG MAN
I can't stand
(Interrupts himself.)

THE YOUNG WOMAN
What is it you can't stand

THE YOUNG MAN
(Looks straight at her.)
You're just lying

THE YOUNG WOMAN
I'm not lying

THE YOUNG MAN
Yes you are
I can tell

THE YOUNG WOMAN
As you like
I'm tired
I want to sleep
(*She drinks wine.*)

THE YOUNG MAN
What you'd really like is to go out again
Go out in that car
and drive around
listen to music
have a nice time
like you say
Or go back to that Baste's house
At least be spared sitting indoors with me
since I never go out
(*He goes right up to her.*)
Go then
Just go out
Go to your precious Baste's house
Do what you want
You don't have to be here
You might as well
go out
go to your precious Baste
or whatever his name is

THE YOUNG WOMAN
(*With an assumed calm.*)
Yes I can go out
Good
(*The YOUNG WOMAN starts walking about the room. The baby begins to cry. The YOUNG MAN starts pushing the pram across the floor, stops, rocks it up and down. The YOUNG WOMAN walks towards the door.*)

THE YOUNG MAN
(*Behind her, surprised, despairing.*)
Are you going

No don't go
I didn't mean it
It's the middle of the night
Don't go
Please
(*The YOUNG WOMAN goes out through the door to the right, and the YOUNG MAN starts walking about the room, rocking the pram, up and down. Lights down. Black.*)

Scene 4

Black. Lights up. Outside the window it is now a bit lighter. The clock shows about four o'clock. The coffee table has been pulled a bit out into the room, and the pram is where the coffee table stood, alongside the sofa. The YOUNG MAN lays on the sofa, looking straight ahead, with one hand rocking the pram up and down. The door to the right opens, the YOUNG WOMAN comes quietly in, with her jacket on, she looks at the YOUNG MAN who is lying there with closed eyes. She goes out through the door to the left. Comes in with a bag, pulls out a drawer in the sideboard and the YOUNG MAN opens his eyes and looks at her.

THE YOUNG MAN
(*Despairing.*)
What are you doing

THE YOUNG WOMAN
So you're awake

THE YOUNG MAN
(*He sits up on the sofa, and the YOUNG WOMAN throws some clothes into a bag.*)
What are you doing

THE YOUNG WOMAN
(*Looks at him.*)
Can't you see
(*The YOUNG MAN gets up.*)

THE YOUNG MAN
No don't
You can't

(*The YOUNG WOMAN pulls out another drawer, takes out some children's clothes, throws them in the bag.*)
Can't you say something
What is it
Say something

THE YOUNG WOMAN
I'm moving out
Can't you see
(*The YOUNG MAN goes and lays down on the sofa again, the YOUNG WOMAN takes the bag with her, goes out through the door to the right, puts the bag down there, comes in again together with BASTE, who is a few years older than the YOUNG MAN.*)

THE YOUNG WOMAN
(*To the YOUNG MAN.*)
So here's Baste
Yes I phoned Baste
(*She laughs briefly.*)
In the middle of the night too
I phoned him
But he came
didn't you
Baste

BASTE
(*Embarrassed.*)
Yes

THE YOUNG MAN
(*Sits up, looks at her confused.*)
No you're joking

THE YOUNG WOMAN
(*Laughs.*)
I'm not joking
I phoned Baste
I can't bear any more of this

THE YOUNG MAN
(*Laughs a little.*)
Lay off now will you

THE YOUNG WOMAN
Alright.
I phoned
And Baste said he'd come
and pick me up
(*Looks at the YOUNG MAN.*)
Do you understand what I'm saying to you

THE YOUNG MAN
(*Uncomprehendingly.*)
No
I don't
You haven't said anything

THE YOUNG WOMAN
I can't bear it any longer
Do you understand what I'm saying to you
I'm leaving
Moving out
Do you understand
Do you understand what I'm saying

THE YOUNG MAN
No I don't

THE YOUNG WOMAN
Do you understand what I'm saying to you
I'm moving out
I can't bear it any more

THE YOUNG MAN
No
don't say that

THE YOUNG WOMAN
(*To BASTE.*)
Could you wait a bit
in the hall
(*BASTE goes out through the door to the hall.*)

THE YOUNG MAN
(*Looks at her.*)
But we're such good friends

No
You mustn't

THE YOUNG WOMAN
It was him
(*Nods to the hall.*)
who gave me the lift
yes it was Baste
this evening
But you must have guessed that
(*Laughs.*)
This evening yes
But you know that
You know that it was him who gave me the lift
Don't you
I've told you
but you don't believe me
it doesn't matter what I say
you still don't believe me
(*Short pause.*)
And surely you understand enough to realise
that it was him I was with
not my girlfriend
Don't you get it
I'll tell you
Baste and I have been
well, fond of each other
I could certainly say
even if it sounds stupid to you
yes Baste and I have been fond of each other
a long time
we have
Just so that you know
(*She laughs.*)

THE YOUNG MAN
But

THE YOUNG WOMAN
It's true
Don't you believe me
Right then

(*Short pause.*)
And in case you're wondering
(*Short pause.*)
Then of course we have made love to each other
several times
this evening we made love in his car
(*The YOUNG MAN stands looking down.*)
Do you hear what I'm saying to you
Or are you completely deaf
Do you get it
Or don't you believe me
Don't you get anything
(*The YOUNG MAN nods. The YOUNG WOMAN goes and sits in the sofa and the YOUNG MAN gets up and starts pushing the pram to and fro across the floor.*
The YOUNG WOMAN turns towards him.)
I can't bear it anymore
Don't you understand
I can't bear it
(*The YOUNG MAN stops, stands rocking the pram up and down.*)
I can't stand it any more
I'm leaving
I'm leaving
I'm off
so now you can go to bed
in peace
(*The YOUNG WOMAN gets up, goes over to the door on the right, calls out.*)
Come in now will you
You don't have to stand out there in the hall waiting
Just come in
(*She turns to the YOUNG MAN.*)
If you don't believe me
come and have a look for yourself
You see here's Baste
There
He's standing out in the hall
And he was in here wasn't he
Didn't you see him
He was right here

Come and look
Come on
come
See for yourself
(*The YOUNG MAN stays where he is.*)
You don't want to
No come on
He's standing there
(*Calls through the door.*)
Come in then
don't just stand there in the hall
(*BASTE comes in and stands in the doorway, he looks at the young man, then BASTE turns round, goes out again. The YOUNG WOMAN looks at the YOUNG MAN.*)
You saw him
didn't you
Now you've seen him twice
It's him I've been with
as you say
we've driven round in his car
Get it
(*The YOUNG MAN just stands rocking the pram up and down. She looks at him.*)
I'm leaving
I can't bear it any more
Don't just stand there
Say something
I can't bear it any more
I'm going now
That's enough now
I can't bear it any more
I'm moving out
(*The YOUNG WOMAN goes out through the door to the right and the YOUNG MAN goes and lies down on the sofa, the child starts screaming, but he just remains lying down. The YOUNG WOMAN and BASTE come in. To BASTE.*)
Could you rock him a bit
and push the pram around
(*BASTE goes over to the pram, starts rocking it up and down and after a while the baby stops crying. The YOUNG WOMAN goes out through the door to the left. The YOUNG*

MAN sits up in the sofa, looks at BASTE where he stands rocking the pram up and down, then BASTE notices that the YOUNG MAN is looking at him and he looks at the YOUNG MAN, they both look down. The YOUNG WOMAN comes in, with one more bottle in her hand. To BASTE.)
I had to fetch a few baby clothes
(*To the YOUNG MAN.*)
I won't take very much with me now
But I'll come back
tomorrow
and pick up the rest
(*The YOUNG WOMAN goes over to the sideboard, pulls out another drawer, takes out some more baby clothes, looks at them, shoves them into the bag. She takes out a little brass bowl from the sideboard, stands looking at it for quite a while, puts it on top of the sideboard.*)
I'll just take a few things with me.
I'll have to pick up the rest later
(*BASTE nods. Pause.
To the YOUNG MAN.*)
Baste and I have known each other
a while
Haven't we
Baste

BASTE
Yes

THE YOUNG MAN
(*From the sofa.*)
A long time

BASTE
A year
perhaps
(*Points to the pushchair.*)
But it's still you that's
the father
You can see that
(*The YOUNG MAN gets up, walks across the room.*)
Are you going to take me now

(*The YOUNG MAN shakes his head, goes over to the window, stands there looking out. The YOUNG WOMAN goes out through the door to the left. Pause.*)
It'll pass
That's the way it goes

THE YOUNG MAN
Yes
(*Pause.*)

BASTE
Yes
It all happened a bit quick
for me too
all this
But
Well
(*The baby starts crying, and BASTE starts rocking the pram up and down.*)
She said you had threatened her
But
(*The child stops screaming.*)

THE YOUNG WOMAN
(*Comes in with a further bag. To BASTE, laughs.*)
Well this is where I've been living
What do you think
(*Laughs.*)
Nice
do you think

BASTE
Yes it's not too bad here
is it

THE YOUNG WOMAN
Yes I got this flat
Him over there
(*Nods towards the YOUNG MAN.*)
he's never done anything
He writes
Did you know

BASTE
(*To the YOUNG MAN.*)
So you write

THE YOUNG WOMAN
And he gets rejected all the time

BASTE
It can't be so easy to write
and get published
can it

THE YOUNG WOMAN
It's just him that thinks
that it's easy
(*Laughs a bit.*)
But he never gets anything published
He just keeps on writing
and complains that the kid is screaming
(*The YOUNG MAN goes out through the door to the left. The YOUNG WOMAN throws her bag down on the floor and stands looking at BASTE. After a while they move towards one another, hug each other, stand and hold each other tight, let go of each other, go and sit on the sofa. The YOUNG MAN comes in through the door, stands in the doorway, looks at them.*)

THE YOUNG MAN
(*Staring ahead he speaks out into the living room.*)
What time are you coming
to get your things

THE YOUNG WOMAN
(*Straightens, looks at him.*)
Well I suppose you're going to kill us
now
him and me
aren't you

THE YOUNG MAN
(*Resignedly.*)
What time are you coming to
get your things

THE YOUNG WOMAN
What a terrible rush
you're in
(*Laughs a little. To BASTE.*)
Can you fetch the things
Hire a van
Tomorrow
can you manage that tomorrow

BASTE
Yes
That should be alright
(*To the YOUNG MAN.*)
What time would suit you
(*The YOUNG MAN shrugs his shoulders.*)
It doesn't matter to you

THE YOUNG WOMAN
It would be nice
if it could be quite soon
I'm thinking of the cot
(*Looks at BASTE.*)
We need that
Maybe you can fetch the things tomorrow

BASTE
(*To the YOUNG MAN.*)
That suit

THE YOUNG MAN
(*Shrugs his shoulders.*)
Yes

BASTE
Sure

THE YOUNG MAN
Yes
(*The YOUNG MAN goes out to the left. Long pause.*)

BASTE
(*To the YOUNG WOMAN.*)
This isn't really the right way

to do this
is it
I suppose
Suddenly
In the middle of the night
or whatever time it is

THE YOUNG WOMAN
But I couldn't bear any more
I couldn't cope any more

BASTE
Yes
(*Short pause.*)
But he

THE YOUNG WOMAN
Don't worry about it
He'll be alright
Or he won't
I can't bear it any more
It's all the same to me

BASTE
He's taking it quite calmly

THE YOUNG WOMAN
Yes

BASTE
Doesn't he care

THE YOUNG WOMAN
I don't know
Frankly I haven't a clue
In some way
he must do
I don't know

BASTE
Can't we get away from here
soon
(*Laughs briefly.*)

I can't believe I dared come up here
I must be really in love
I'm certainly mad anyway

THE YOUNG WOMAN
Me too
(*She kisses him on the cheek.*)
I can't bear being where you are not
I think of you all the time
I have to be where you are
It had to be
(*Short pause.*)
It had to
(*Short pause.*)
And his parents
(*She shakes her head.*)
they're absolutely dreadful
And he's exactly like them
Exactly the same
Just as clumsy
and helpless
His father just sat there
(*Looks at the armchair.*)
and stared dead ahead with confused eyes

BASTE
Can't we go

THE YOUNG WOMAN
Alright
(*Looks at BASTE, smiles.*)
I'm so fond of you

BASTE
And now you and I are going to be together
Aren't we

THE YOUNG WOMAN
Yes

BASTE
And you must never abandon me
You must never go away from me

Yes I mean it
You must never leave me
like you're leaving him now

THE YOUNG WOMAN
Never never
I promise
I shall never abandon you
I shall always be with you
Always
(*Short pause.*)
But can't we go now

BASTE
Because if you leave me
Well then I don't know
what I'll do

THE YOUNG WOMAN
I won't leave you
Ever
But you know that.
I'll never leave you
(*Short pause.*)
And you must never leave me
either

BASTE
But can't we go now
We can't stay here any longer
We must go
(*BASTE gets up. She nods, but remains sitting. He goes and stretches his arms out to her, but she remains sitting, not taking his hands.*)
You can't change your mind now
What's wrong with you

THE YOUNG WOMAN
I have to pack a bit more
(*She gets up, goes and picks up one of the bags, goes over to the sideboard, pulls out a drawer. She takes out a photo album, opens it.*)

BASTE
(*Laughs briefly.*)
No
This is not the time
to look at photographs
not now
(*She closes the photo album, puts it down in her bag.*)
Listen
All that
yeah
we can fetch it later
Can't you just bring with you
the bare essentials
Tomorrow
or another day
we can come
and fetch all that other stuff
can't we
(*She nods. She goes over and takes the brass bowl she had put on top of the sideboard, stands weighing it in her hands, looks at it.*)
Can't we do that
It's late
(*She nods, puts the brass bowl in her bag.*)
We'll fetch the rest later

THE YOUNG WOMAN
(*Nods.*)
Yes

BASTE
Just bring with you the bare essentials
now yeah
(*She nods again.*)
And we can get away from here
It's late
And
Well
(*Short pause.*)
well I'm thinking of him a bit
well
you know

(*She nods, goes over to the sideboard, pulls out a further drawer, takes out a table cloth, looks at it, puts it back. She sees the picture of the little boy which hangs on the wall, she takes down the picture, stands looking at it, and then lays that in her bag too, stands and looks around.*)

THE YOUNG WOMAN
It's so odd
this
the things are kind of pulling at me
(*She laughs.*)

BASTE
Can't we just
well get going
We
(*Short pause.*)
Well we don't need to drag it out
all this
Can't we just

THE YOUNG WOMAN
(*Nods.*)
Yes
But
It's so strange that it should have
turned out like this

BASTE
No come on
Don't be silly

THE YOUNG WOMAN
We have
(*Nods backwards with her head.*)
lived quite a long while together
him and me
Had a child together
as well
Yes
You do understand that
Bought ourselves things

together
not so many things
but some
It probably would have been simpler
if we'd had many things
not just a few
some pictures
bowls
tablecloths
a few quite simple things
is all we have
That's why

BASTE
Come on now

THE YOUNG WOMAN
Just now
Well it feels so sad
everything is so wrong
I kind of want to cry
Everything
No
don't listen to me
I'm just talking
That brass bowl
(*Points to the bag.*)
is the saddest thing I've seen
(*She nods at him.*)
Yes, it's true
(*Pause.*)
Everything is so
Well I don't know

BASTE
Don't be silly now
It was you who phoned

THE YOUNG WOMAN
Yes I know
But
And I know that you and I

(*Looks at him.*)
belong together
there's no doubt about that
but him and me
(*Short pause.*)
He has always been kind to me
(*Looks at BASTE.*)
Yes he has
And he's been very nice to the kid
taken care of him a lot
and he was there at the birth
helped me all he could
Yes
And so
(*She covers her face with her hands.*)

BASTE
Do you want me to go

THE YOUNG WOMAN
(*Removes her hands from her face, looks at him.*)
No no
Don't go
I can't bear it
I miss you so
when you're not
here
I can't bear it
You mustn't go
(*BASTE goes and sits on the sofa. The YOUNG WOMAN goes and sits in the armchair.*)
That's just the way it is
Oh it's so miserable and sad
Everything is so dreadful
It happened so quickly
Something always just happens
Do you know that
(*She looks at BASTE.*)
Do you know that
that something or other always just happens
I don't like that something happens

I'd rather everything was calm
and that just the usual things
things you're used to
would happen
But then something unusual always happens
Always
(*She drinks some wine.*)
I don't know what it is
that always makes something happen
But it must be something
Because something always happens
I don't want anything to happen
and then something
happens all the same
(*Looks at BASTE.*)
What is it that makes everything happen
Is it me
Something else

BASTE
I don't know
But can't we go
We can can talk later

THE YOUNG WOMAN
(*Tearful.*)
Yes
(*Pause.*)
Do you know what I'm thinking about
(*He shakes his head.*)
I'm so stupid
I'm thinking about the saucepans
out there in the kitchen
(*Resignedly.*)
I'm thinking that I am just about to leave
the saucepans in the kitchen
That's what I'm thinking about
I'm completely mad

BASTE
(*A trace of resignation.*)
Do you want to

or do you not want to
leave
You have to
(*Interrupts himself, looks at her.*)
Well you have to
You and I have to
be together
we have to
don't we
(*The YOUNG WOMAN nods.*)
Don't we
Come on
Let's go

THE YOUNG WOMAN
(*Gets up, dries her tears, she laughs a bit.*)
It's so sad
Everything is so sad

BASTE
Come on then

THE YOUNG WOMAN
I seem to be sobering up

BASTE
No don't be silly
We've talked
so often about it
It's nearly done now
All you have to do now is go
Come on then
Come on
(*She nods.*)
That's it come on
(*She walks around a little in the living room, looks at the sideboard, goes over to the pram, peeps down at the child.*)

THE YOUNG WOMAN
(*Quietly, to BASTE.*)
He's sleeping so sweetly
Have you seen

how sweetly he's sleeping
Come and look
(*BASTE gets up, goes over to her, peeps down at the child.*)

BASTE
Yes he's sleeping
nice and quietly now

THE YOUNG WOMAN
I think he was quite unsettled tonight

BASTE
(*Questioningly.*)
He told you that
(*She nods.*)

THE YOUNG WOMAN
(*To the child.*)
And now we two are going to move
Live somewhere else
And you
(*Looks at BASTE.*)
in one way become his father
(*BASTE nods. Pause. To BASTE, suddenly.*)
No I can't go now
I can't
He
(*Short pause.*)
he's always been kind to me
He didn't know the good he could have done
And then he's so helpless
daren't go out
days can pass without him daring to go out
he doesn't even dare
go to the shop
And then this writing of his
Completely hopeless
everything he writes.
I'm sure that it's hopeless
The only thing he reckons he can manage
is to sit indoors writing
But of course no-one wants to publish

what he writes
He's not good enough
He's no good at all
Was useless at school
Failed several subjects
We were at school together
Well you know
I've already told you
I've known him since secondary school
We've been together
since then
(*She looks at BASTE.*)
until now
at least nearly
yes
(*Pause.*)
He's alright
but he doesn't understand anything
(*She laughs briefly.*)
It's me
who's had to organise everything
(*Short pause.*)
Him on his own
(*She shakes her head, looks at BASTE.*)
I can't go
It's really ridiculous
but I can't go
It's no good

BASTE
But then you can't
(*Interrupts himself.*)
Us then

THE YOUNG WOMAN
I don't know
I'm fond of you
I'm in love with you
I can't live
well it feels like I can't
without you

But I don't know
I can't leave
either
Not now
at any rate.
I don't know

BASTE
When will we meet
then

THE YOUNG WOMAN
I don't know
We have to meet I suppose
(*BASTE goes to the door to the right, stops.*)
No don't go

BASTE
You have to make up your mind

THE YOUNG WOMAN
I'll stay
(*BASTE stops, stands and stares at the floor.*)
I don't know.
I miss you already
but I can see
that I can't go
either
Not like this
at any rate.
I don't know

BASTE
Then it's probably best
we don't see each other anymore
It all just goes wrong

THE YOUNG WOMAN
(*Quickly goes to him.*)
No don't say that
You mustn't say that
We have to meet
I'm so fond of you

BASTE
Well come on then
Decide
This is no good
this
It's madness
Come on
(*She stands looking down.*)
You're not coming
(*She shakes her head.*)
Okay
Then I'll
go then
(*He looks at her entreatingly.*)
Won't you come
(*Entreatingly.*)
Come
(*She stands looking down. Long pause.*)
Well then I'll go
(*She nods.*)
Can't you come
(*She shakes her head.*)
Well then I'd better just go I suppose

THE YOUNG WOMAN
Yes

BASTE
If he
(*Nods towards the door to the left.*)
goes along with all this
well then

THE YOUNG WOMAN
I don't know

BASTE
Then I'll go then
(*He looks at her, as if he were waiting for her to say something.*)
You don't love me
not enough
at any rate

That's
at least
good to know

THE YOUNG WOMAN
That's not it
either
And you know it

BASTE
Then at least I know
that
(*A loud shot from a rifle is heard. The YOUNG WOMAN looks at BASTE in terror, BASTE jumps. Horrified.*)
He's shot himself
I think he's bloody shot himself
It was a shot
I heard a shot
I think he's shot himself
Listen
(*He goes and nudges the YOUNG WOMAN, who stands there no longer following.*)
Go on
You have to go and see
see if he's shot himself
It was a shot
Go on
Call him anyway
You have to do something
(*The YOUNG WOMAN walks slowly across the room, and out left. BASTE stands stiffly looking after her. She comes in again, nods.*)
He's shot himself
(*She nods again. Burst out loudly.*)
He's shot himself

THE YOUNG WOMAN
(*Very quietly.*)
There's only a little bit left
of his head
(*She starts crying.*)

BASTE

We must
(*The child starts crying.*)
He's shot himself
I
Well
We must
I don't really know
I can go and phone the police
A doctor
I'll phone
(*He goes out through the door to the right.*)

THE YOUNG WOMAN

(*Calls after him.*)
Don't go
(*Long pause. Lights down. The baby gradually stops crying. Black.*)

The End.